THE
WOMAN'S DAY
BOOK OF
DELICIOUS DESSERTS

Edited by

JULIE
HOUSTON

FAWCETT COLUMBINE • **NEW YORK**

THE WOMAN'S DAY BOOK OF DELICIOUS DESSERTS

Published by Fawcett Columbine Books, CBS Educational and
Professional Publishing, a division of CBS Inc.

ISBN: 0-449-90061-4

All photography by Woman's Day Studio

Printed in the United States of America

First Fawcett Columbine printing: November 1981

10 9 8 7 6 5 4 3 2 1

CONTENTS

EDITOR'S INTRODUCTION

It can be the simplest everyday supper or a gala special banquet—what leaves a lasting impression of the food that is served at any meal is dessert.

More than just delicious, desserts have a miraculous way of lifting spirits, easing the cares of the day and leaving us with a peaceful feeling of appreciation for family, friends and the pleasures of good eating. For if good food is meant to please, then dessert can surely be described as pure bliss—whether it be a colorful fruit compote or a three-tiered chocolate layer cake.

A good cook plans dessert to complement the meal, to insure the comfort and pleasure of those who will be dining together at the table. In choosing a dessert, there are several factors to consider. Is the meal heavy or light? If the food is substantial and filling, then a light, delicately flavored dessert is called for—sponge cake instead of pound cake, for example, or fruit pie rather than cream pie, simple custard or sherbet rather than rich mousse or ice cream. Is the weather stifling hot, or the main dish spicy? An icy-cold frozen dessert can do wonders to cool and refresh the palate—and the spirit.

A dessert that is planned with thought and care is guaranteed to be a triumph, reaping the highest praise. Moreover, it is no surprise that many a host or hostess's reputation has been built on desserts—the last course served but, when perfectly suited for the meal, the first remembered.

Woman's Day magazine has built much of its own fine reputation for good foods on its dessert recipes, always high in quality and totally reliable for producing the finest, most delectable results.

Going back over decades of recipes that appeared in the magazine, it was surprising to see the constant *variety* of desserts offered month after month.

This actually became the very basis of the book—with over *thirty* main categories of desserts represented, from layer cakes, small loaf cakes, tortes, cake rolls, fruit pies, chocolate pies, tarts, cheesecakes, cream puffs and crêpes, to puddings, custards, fresh fruits, ice cream, sherbet and frozen soufflés. All in all, there are over 250 recipes from which to make the perfect dessert choice for every possible menu.

In addition to the individual desserts, the book also provides easy access to highly creative cooking, with general suggestions throughout for combining certain elements—cakes with different fillings, pies with toppings or crusts, for example—to suit one's own tastes. To make these new combinations easier to choose, chapters 17–19 contain all of the recipes for pastry, pie crusts, frostings, fillings, sauces, toppings, garnishes and such, called for in specific recipes, and then go a step further by including scores of others in these areas that appeared in the magazine and were just too good to leave out.

Complete with all the basic techniques for making perfect desserts, filled with useful tips and hints for success, no matter what one's level of expertise in the kitchen, *The Woman's Day Book of Delicious Desserts* is a treasured collection of time-tested recipes for the most delectable, unforgettable desserts ever—a cookbook to use again and again when only the best will do.

Julie Houston,
Editor

1
THE DESSERT-MAKER'S KITCHEN

Ingredients

There are certain ingredients basic to dessert-making; most of these are included below. Wherever possible, tips and techniques that pertain to specific ingredients have also been included in this chapter. Regarding *all* ingredients, there is really only one rule to follow for great, memorable desserts: Don't scrimp. Use only the freshest, finest ingredients you can buy.

Butter. There are many cooks who are of the opinion that no shortening can replace the rich, distinctive flavor that sweet butter imparts to a dessert, whether it be a cake, pudding or pie. But this is simply a matter of taste. If salted butter is used, omit the salt, if called for, from the list of ingredients. Most recipes give adequate results when margarine is used instead of butter. Others are traditionally made with vegetable oil. Frozen desserts, and their sauces, usually call for oil wherever shortening is needed. In these cases, heavy cream and/or eggs impart a rich, full flavor.

Eggs. Eggs have such a temperamental reputation that many people shy away from the simplest recipes if anything more than dropping a whole egg in the batter is required. Granted, eggs—and how they are handled—are a crucial element in most of the finest desserts. But there is no need to be intimidated. There is nothing mysterious about eggs once the basic techniques have been experienced.

Use large-grade eggs in desserts. When using whole eggs in cakes, lightly stir eggs and sugar together for less than a minute, and then rest the bowl over—but not touching—a pan of simmering water. This is a trick used by the best professional dessert-makers, who know very well that temperature affects the performance of an egg, particularly when baking a light, delicate cake. This warming procedure encourages fluffier, lighter eggs with more volume when beaten. Heat the eggs to a point just slightly warmer than lukewarm (not more than two or three minutes, depending on the thickness of the bowl). Then beat them with an electric mixer or rotary blender until very thick, fluffy and cool. Use this trick no matter what the cake recipe, and the eggs will add immensely to improving the texture.

Whole eggs and separated egg yolks are frequently used to thicken sauces and sweet custards. Eggs *do* curdle when overheated, but it is very easy to prevent this from happening with the following procedure: Heat up all sauce or custard ingredients *before* adding eggs. Rapidly stir a few spoonfuls of the hot mixture into the eggs to warm them, and then add them to the pan, stirring constantly and cooking over low heat or in a double boiler until the mixture is thickened. It should coat a spoon well when it is thick enough to use. An added safety measure to avoid curdling—keep a bowl of cold water near the stove. If you have a fleeting thought that the eggs are curdling, immediately cool the mixture by dunking the bottom of the saucepan into the bowl of water. This almost always works to save the sauce, and somehow, keeping the bowl nearby gives an air of confidence to the whole procedure.

Separated egg whites should be brought to room temperature or slightly warmer and beaten until soft-peaked and fluffy.

Unless the recipe requires it, it is not necessary to beat yolks more than a minute or so, particularly if they are to be added to other ingredients without first being combined with sugar.

Cream. Use fresh heavy cream for whipping. If possible, avoid ultrapasteurized cream, which has a cloying, somewhat chalky flavor when whipped. Heavy cream, the bowl and utensils used for whipping should all be very cold.

Flour. Use exactly what is called for. Usually that is all-purpose white flour, but cake flours, which contain a blend of flour and starch, will produce a lighter cake than white flour when baking powder is used as leavening. In cakes leavened with eggs, it makes little difference which is used.

Sugars and sweeteners. To assure accurate flavor and texture, use exactly what is called for in the recipe. Honey or light corn syrup is often used in frozen desserts, where sugar would be difficult to dissolve. Keep a box of confectioners' sugar on hand for icings and for dusting certain cakes before serving. "Vanilla Sugar" is easy to prepare and adds a distinctive flavor to many recipes. Simply enclose a split vanilla bean in a covered container with granulated or confectioners' sugar and let it sit twenty-four hours or more. It will keep indefinitely.

Many fancy cakes and other desserts call for sugar syrups, whereby the sugar is dissolved and cooked to varying degrees—from a heavy syrup (at 230°F.), called "the thread stage" because the slightly cooled syrup will form a two-inch thread when extended between thumb and forefinger; to brown, caramelized sugar, at 320°F. No matter what stage, the trick in dissolving sugar is to do it *very* slowly and thoroughly over low heat, stirring constantly. It does no good to rush the process—one grain of undissolved sugar can crystallize the whole batch when cooled. Once thoroughly dissolved, the syrup can then be cooked as specified in the recipe.

Nuts. A wide variety of nuts is used in desserts, either as a flavorful main ingredient or a pleasing finishing touch, on cakes or molded desserts, for example. The flavor of nuts, whether they be almonds, walnuts, filberts or pecans, adds an unmistakable element of pleasure, texture and plain good taste to just about any dessert.

To save money, buy nuts in quantity and store them in the refrigerator. Shelled nuts can be frozen for many months without losing flavor. It is useful to know the following about certain types of nuts:

Almonds should be shelled and then blanched to remove skins. To do this easily, cover the nuts with boiling water, let stand five minutes and then slip skins off with the fingers.

To skin filberts or hazelnuts (as they are called interchangeably), put them in a baking dish in a single layer and place it in a 350°F. oven for fifteen minutes, or until the skins are dark brown. Cool slightly and then rub together in a towel or between hands to remove skins.

Shelled Brazil nuts can be skinned with a vegetable peeler and then peeled further into thin shavings to use as decorative garnishes or in place of coconut for accent.

To crush nuts, toast them very lightly in the oven, just to heat them through a few minutes, and then use a rolling pin to crush, taking care not to reduce the pieces into fine bits.

To pulverize or grind nuts, use a food processor or blender.

Chocolate. There are many ways to substitute one kind of chocolate for another in baking and cooking, but for the most accurate flavor derived from following a recipe, use what is called for—sweet, bittersweet, semisweet; solid bars, chips or cocoa powder. When melting chocolate, use a double boiler; place the chocolate over the water—but it should be water that has been brought to a boil and then turned off—not actively boiling water. Cover the pan and let the chocolate melt. Fifteen minutes or so is about all that is needed if the pieces are about one inch square.

Dried Fruits. Raisins, currants, dates and other dried fruits should be softened before use. If they are dry and hard, they will not soften up when folded into most dessert batters or mixes. Most dried fruit should be soaked in hot water for at least an hour or more, drained, and dried with paper towels. One favored method of plumping dried fruits, particularly golden or dark raisins, is to heat them in sweet wine, brandy or water, allow to stand ten minutes and then drain well. This brings out flavor.

Citrus Fruits. As with all fresh fruits, use plump, well-formed lemons, oranges, limes and other citrus fruits.

Lemons and limes yield more juice if warmed in hot water a few minutes or rolled on a hard surface before squeezing.

There are as many dessert lovers who crave citrus flavors as there are chocolate addicts, and yet it is a chore to mince or grate lemons, limes and such. To make it easier, prepare zest from these fruits in quantity, ahead of time. Use a vegetable peeler to peel zest (the thin colored outer skin only, and not the white pulp). The zest from three to four medium oranges or five to six lemons or limes will yield about a scant three-quarters of a cup when grated on a medium-fine blade or chopped neatly in very fine lengths. Store the zest, covered tightly, in the refrigerator. Any left over from one dessert recipe can be used in another—sprinkled over fruits, custards, ice cream, for example.

Coconut. Fresh coconut is infinitely more tasty than canned, which tends to be oversweetened and processed. If you have a food processor, it takes almost no time at all to prepare an ample supply of fresh coconut, to use immediately or store in the freezer (in an airtight container) for later use. If frozen, thaw completely before using; very little flavor will have been lost. Coconut is so good when fresh that even using a hand shredder makes the job worthwhile, particularly when coconuts are in season and at their lowest price.

Using a hammer and chisel or pick, make a hole in each of the three indentations, the "eyes," at the base of the coconut and drain off the milk for another use. Place the coconut in a 350°F. oven for fifteen to thirty minutes, until the shell cracks. Remove the coconut from the oven, tap all over with a hammer and then break open. Pry out coconut meat and peel off the dark outer skin with a vegetable peeler. To prepare meat, use the shredding disk of a food processor or the medium side of a hand grater. One coconut yields about one and a half to two cups of shredded meat. When measuring, pack lightly in a cup.

To toast freshly grated or canned coconut, spread it out thinly in a shallow baking pan. Put in moderate oven (350°F.) and toast eight minutes or until delicately browned. Stir coconut or shake pan often to toast evenly.

When used as a garnish, many people prefer to tint coconut rather than use it plain. An easy way to do this is to put one to two tablespoons of any fruit-flavor gelatin and one and a third cups flaked coconut in a one-quart jar. Cover tightly and shake until the coconut is evenly tinted.

Basic Procedures

In addition to many of the procedures given in the previous section (i.e., those pertaining to specific ingredients) and within each individual recipe, there are several techniques which help to produce perfect desserts. All of the procedures described here will pertain to cakes; several others—folding and whipping, for example—are useful in preparing frozen desserts, souffles, mousses, sauces and more.

In almost all dessert-making, a light, efficient hand is all-important.

To cream shortening, blend it with the sugar called for in the recipe until everything is light in color and creamy in texture. With ingredients at room temperature, it only takes a few minutes to cream butter, and it is important not to overblend, which would cause the butter mixture to separate and the cake to become coarse.

Mixing. If you are mixing by hand, begin at the center of the bowl and work out in round, even strokes. Take care not to mix any more than just to combine ingredients. There is not much to it; the expert hand knows when to stop.

Folding is the gentlest way to combine ingredients, particularly those that have been whipped first to retain air. To fold, use one motion to bring a rubber spatula straight down through the center of the mass, turn the spatula up against the side of the bowl, out over the mass and down again through the center. Turn the bowl slightly (one quarter of the way around) with each fold. Many experts fold ingredients by hand, keeping fingers spread slightly as they dip the hand straight down into the bowl, up and around the sides, picking up and folding in portions of batter, one handful at a time.

Sifting not only gets lumps out of flour and other dry ingredients but also adds air. If a recipe specifies sifting, do it if you want to be sure of a fine, delicate cake.

Equipment

It seems that as a cook's experience grows, so do the contents of the kitchen cabinet: The wider the range of desserts mastered, the more equipment tends to accumulate. Listed below are some of the basics that are convenient to have on hand. While all of these items are not absolutely necessary—at least until called for in a recipe—they make up a fairly complete supply of kitchen equipment for the dessert maker.

Baking Pans. Most aluminum or glass baking pans come in standard sizes, marked on the bottom. There are cake recipes in this book calling for pan sizes on the following list, which also includes guidelines for serving amounts:

8- or 9-inch round pan	12 to 16 servings (2-layer cake)
8- or 9-inch square pan	9 to 12 servings
9 x 5 x 3-inch loaf pan	9 to 12 servings
13 x 9 x 2-inch oblong pan	12 to 15 servings
9- or 10-inch tube pan	12 to 16 servings
9- or 10-inch fluted Bundt pan	12 to 16 servings
15 x 10 x 1-inch jellyroll pan	8 to 10 servings

Many cake batters, particularly those using shortening and baking powder or baking soda, can be baked in pans other than what is called for, but making substitutions can get you into trouble. Unless the recipe gives alternatives, it is best to use the type of pan described.

For pies, the amount of filling determines the size pan. The standard size is nine inches in diameter, serving eight to ten portions of pie.

Soufflé dishes, glass or ceramic, are suitable for not only soufflés but also mousses, puddings and pudding cakes.

Tart pans and cheesecake pans (the latter also referred to as springform pans for the spring mechanism that releases the side from the bottom of the pan) are both most convenient when the bottom is removable.

Baking sheets, for cream puffs and éclairs.

Tin molds and tin trays, for frozen desserts, come in a range of shapes and sizes. As for utensils, the list could go on and on but should include: a set of three mixing bowls, wooden mixing spoons, long and short wire whisks, hand-held grater, and juicer.

2
LAYER CAKES

For special occasions the year round, nothing is more gloriously all-American than layer cake—moist, light-textured and high as the hopes of all who share the celebration of a birthday, anniversary, graduation, job promotion or any other special occasion.

Season after season, *Woman's Day* has offered an unsurpassed choice of big, beautiful layer cakes to its readers. From the Tender Chocolate Layer Cake and the Almond-Mocha Cake to the Orange-Coconut Cake and Meringue Cake Supreme, the recipes presented here accurately reflect the diversity of taste and texture and unanimous appeal of this all-time favorite dessert.

It is easy to split a single layer cake into several layers (and this applies to loaf cakes in other sections of this book). Measure out the height of each layer you want, with a ruler held perpendicular to the cake. Mark the measurements with toothpicks, all the way around the edge of the cake, at three or four intervals.

Use the toothpicks as a cutting guide. Plain sewing thread will easily cut through plain cake layers. Hold the thread taut and draw it through the cake where indicated by the picks. Use a serrated knife to cut through nut cakes or those with dried fruit in the batter.

Because most of these layer cakes are made with shortening (those without appear in Chapter 8), they are easy to frost and fill because they are denser and more finely grained than delicate, airy sponge cakes. If filling is soft and the layers slide, use metal skewers or extra long wooden matches (often called fireplace matches) to anchor layers one on top of the other while frosting.

Remove picks or skewers when cake has set or just before serving.

Different fillings and frostings (see Chapter 18) will transform any cake presented here into something entirely new, exciting and equally delicious.

TENDER CHOCOLATE LAYER CAKE

*Rich, handsome and impressive—the fulfillment of a
chocolate lover's dream.*

2¼ cups flour
1 teaspoon baking powder
½ teaspoon each, baking soda
　and salt
¾ cup butter or margarine,
　softened
1½ cups sugar
2 eggs
1 teaspoon vanilla

2 squares (2 ounces)
　unsweetened chocolate,
　melted and cooled
1 cup cool water
Dark-Chocolate Butter Frosting
　(page 143)
Shaved or chopped semisweet
　chocolate (optional)

Stir together flour, baking powder, baking soda and salt; set aside. In large bowl of mixer cream butter, sugar, eggs and vanilla at high speed until fluffy, about 5 minutes, scraping bowl occasionally. Stir in melted chocolate. At low speed stir in flour mixture alternately with water until well blended. Pour into 2 greased 9-inch layer-cake pans lined with waxed paper. Bake in preheated 350°F. oven 30 minutes or until pick inserted in center comes out clean. Cool in pans on racks 10 minutes, then invert on rack, peel off paper, turn layers top side up and cool. Wrap airtight and store in cool place up to 5 days or freeze. Before serving, fill and frost with Dark-Chocolate Butter Frosting. Swirl top in decorative pattern and garnish side with shaved chocolate. Serves 12. **NOTE:** Refrigerate any left over.

CHOCOLATE-RUM LAYERS

*Frost with a favorite frosting or one chosen from
Chapter 18.*

⅔ cup butter or margarine,
　softened
1⅓ cups granulated sugar
3 eggs
2 ounces unsweetened chocolate
　and ⅓ cup semisweet
　chocolate pieces, melted and
　cooled

2 teaspoons rum extract
2 cups all-purpose flour
1 teaspoon baking soda
½ teaspoon salt
1 cup milk

Cream butter; gradually add sugar, and cream until light and fluffy. Add eggs, one at a time, beating thoroughly after each. Blend in chocolate and rum extract. Add sifted dry ingredients alternately with milk, blending after each addition until smooth. Pour into 2 greased and floured 9-inch layer cake pans. Bake in preheated 350°F. oven 25 minutes or until done. Cool on rack 5 minutes, then turn out and cool. Fill and frost as desired.

CHOCOLATE SHADOW CAKE

Dark, velvety cake with rich chocolate flavor, topped with butter cream frosting and semisweet-chocolate shadow.

4 squares unsweetened chocolate	1 teaspoon baking soda
1½ cups sugar	½ teaspoon salt
½ cup butter, softened	⅔ cup milk
1 teaspoon vanilla	Butter cream Frosting (page 142)
3 eggs	Chocolate Shadow
2 cups sifted cake flour	

Melt chocolate in ½ cup hot water in top part of double boiler, over hot water. Cook, stirring, until thickened. Add ½ cup sugar and cook, stirring, 2 to 3 minutes. Remove from water and cool. Cream butter, then gradually add remaining sugar and cream until light and fluffy. Add vanilla; add eggs, one at a time, beating thoroughly after each. Add chocolate mixture and blend well. Fold in sifted dry ingredients alternately with milk, beginning and ending with flour mixture. Pour into two 9-inch layer pans lined on bottom with waxed paper. Bake in moderate oven (350°F.) 30 to 35 minutes or until cake tester comes out clean. Cool in pans 5 minutes, then turn out on cake racks to cool thoroughly. Spread frosting between layers and on top and sides of cake. Pour Chocolate Shadow over top, allowing some to run down sides of cake. Let chocolate set before cutting.

CHOCOLATE SHADOW Melt ½ cup semisweet chocolate pieces in top of double boiler over hot water. Blend in 3 to 4 tablespoons warm water, or enough to make mixture smooth and thin enough to pour.

CHERRY-CHOCOLATE CAKE

Génoise layers, frosting and filling are flavored with cocoa. This favorite is also known as Black Forest Cake.

6 eggs, separated	Cocoa Whipped-Cream Frosting (page 149)
¾ cup sugar	1 can (17 ounces) pitted dark
1 teaspoon vanilla	sweet cherries, well drained,
½ cup cocoa mixed well with ⅓ cup flour	halved, then drained again (see Note)
½ cup butter or margarine, melted and cooled	Chocolate Curls (page 155)

In large bowl of mixer beat egg whites at medium speed until soft peaks form. Increase to high speed and gradually beat in sugar until stiff peaks form; set aside. Stir vanilla into egg yolks to break up and blend. Fold about ¼ egg-white mixture into yolks; pour over remaining egg-white mixture. Sprinkle with a few tablespoons cocoa mixture at a time, folding in gently but thoroughly after each addition. Fold in only clear part of melted butter, discarding milky residue. Divide batter evenly among 3 well-greased or paper-lined 8-inch layer pans. Bake on center rack in preheated 350°F. oven 25 minutes or until pick inserted in center comes out clean. Run small spatula around edge of layers, invert on racks and peel off paper; cool. Prepare frosting. Remove 1 cup and fold in cherries; spread between layers, stacking. Frost top and side of cake with remaining frosting. Decorate with Chocolate Curls. Chill at least 2 hours before serving. Serves 8 to 10. **NOTE:** When available, substitute 1 pound fresh ripe dark cherries, pitted, halved and soaked in rum overnight.

ALMOND-MOCHA CAKE

(color plate 3, top)
Tender almond Génoise *layers frosted with mocha butter cream*

8 eggs, separated
¾ cup sugar
½ teaspoon almond extract
¾ cup ground blanched almonds
½ cup flour

⅓ cup butter or margarine, melted and cooled
Mocha Butter cream (recipe page 143)
Toasted slivered or sliced almonds and Chocolate Curls (page 155)

In large bowl of mixer beat egg whites at medium speed until soft peaks form. Increase to high speed and gradually beat in sugar until stiff peaks form; set aside. Stir almond extract into egg yolks to break up and blend. Fold about ¼ egg-white mixture into yolks; pour over remaining egg-white mixture. Sprinkle with a few tablespoons each, almonds and flour, at a time, folding in gently but thoroughly after each addition. Fold in only clear part of melted butter, discarding milky residue. Divide batter evenly among 3 greased paper-lined 8-inch layer pans. Bake on center rack in preheated 350°F. oven 20 to 25 minutes or until tops are golden and pick inserted in center comes out clean. Run small spatula around edge of layers, invert on racks and peel off paper; cool. Reserving ½ cup butter cream for decoration, spread about ¾ cup between layers, stacking. Frost top and side of cake with remaining butter cream. Pipe or spoon small dollops of reserved ½ cup butter cream around rim of cake. Garnish center with almonds and Chocolate Curls. Chill at least 2 hours or overnight. Bring to room temperature before serving. Serves 8 to 10.

ORANGE-COCONUT CAKE

*The flavors of citrus and coconut merge together in an
unbeatable combination.*

3 cups cake flour
2¼ teaspoons baking powder
¼ teaspoon salt
4 eggs, separated
2 cups sugar
1 cup butter or margarine,
  softened

½ teaspoon almond extract
1 cup milk
Orange Filling (page 150)
¼ teaspoon almond extract
Boiled Frosting (page 142)
2 cups grated fresh or packaged
  flaked coconut

Stir together flour, baking powder and salt; set aside. In large bowl of electric mixer beat
egg whites until foamy; add ½ cup sugar gradually and beat until stiff but not dry; set
aside. In large bowl of electric mixer cream butter and remaining 1½ cups sugar until light
and fluffy. Add egg yolks and almond extract and beat thoroughly. Stir in flour mixture
alternately with milk until smooth and well blended. Fold in egg-white mixture gently
but thoroughly. Divide batter among 3 greased and floured 9-inch layer-cake pans. Bake
in preheated 350°F. oven about 25 minutes or until golden brown and pick inserted in
center comes out clean. Cool pans on racks 5 minutes, then invert on racks, turning layers
top side up. Cool thoroughly. To assemble cake, spread filling between layers. Beat almond
extract into Boiled Frosting and spread on top and sides of cake. With small spatula make
deep swirls in frosting. Sprinkle with coconut.

LANE CAKE

*This is a basic, delicious white cake that can be filled
and frosted as desired.*

3 cups all-purpose flour
1 tablespoon baking powder
8 egg whites
¼ teaspoon salt
2 cups sugar, divided
1 cup butter or margarine,
  softened

1 teaspoon vanilla
1 cup milk
Bourbon Filling (page 147)
Boiled Frosting (page 142)
Candied fruits (optional)

Stir together flour and baking powder; set aside. In large bowl of mixer beat egg whites
and salt until foamy; gradually add ½ cup sugar and beat until stiff but not dry; set aside.

Cream butter, the remaining 1½ cups sugar and vanilla until light; stir in flour mixture alternately with milk until smooth and well blended. Fold in egg-white mixture gently but thoroughly. Divide batter evenly among 3 greased and floured 9-inch layer-cake pans. Bake in preheated 350°F. oven 20 to 25 minutes or until golden brown and pick inserted in center comes out clean. Cool pans on racks 5 minutes, then invert on racks and turn layers top side up. Cool thoroughly. To assemble cake, spread Bourbon Filling between layers. Frost top and sides with Boiled Frosting. With small spatula make deep swirls in frosting. Decorate with candied fruits. Makes 12 servings. **NOTE:** Cake can be filled 1 week ahead. Wrap air-tight and store in cool place. Frost day of serving. Any white frosting can be used.

BANANA CREAM LAYER CAKE

All ingredients should be at room temperature.

1½ cups sifted cake flour	Sugar
1½ teaspoons baking powder	Lemon juice
½ teaspoon salt	1 cup heavy cream, whipped and
Grated rind of ½ lemon	sweetened
3 eggs, separated	3 fully ripe medium bananas,
	sliced

Sift first 3 ingredients together 3 times. Add ¾ cup cold water and the lemon rind to egg yolks and beat with rotary beater or electric mixer until tripled in volume. Add 1 cup plus 2 tablespoons sugar, a few tablespoons at a time, beating well after each addition. Then add sifted dry ingredients, a small amount at a time, beating slowly and gently with beater. Beat egg whites until foamy, add 1½ teaspoons lemon juice and 3 tablespoons sugar and continue beating until mixture stands in soft peaks. Fold into flour mixture. Pour batter into 2 ungreased round 9-inch layer-cake pans 1½ inches deep. Bake in moderate oven (350°F.) 25 to 30 minutes. Turn upside down on cake racks and let stand until cold. Remove from pans. Just before serving, spread half the whipped cream on one layer of cake. Cover with banana slices dipped in lemon juice. Top with remaining cake layer and decorate with whipped cream and bananas. **NOTE:** For a small family, reserve 1 cake layer for another meal. Cut remaining layer in half and fill with cream and bananas.

TWO-LAYER LADY BALTIMORE CAKE

A fruity, festive layer cake for the holiday season.

1⅓ cups cake flour
2 teaspoons baking powder
3 egg whites (about ½ cup)
⅛ teaspoon salt
1 cup sugar
½ cup butter or margarine,
  softened

1 teaspoon vanilla
½ cup cold milk
Dried Fruits Frosting (page 145)
Whole candied red cherries
Candied green pineapple, cut in
  small pieces
Nut halves

Stir flour and baking powder together; set aside. In large bowl of electric mixer beat egg whites with salt until foamy; add ¼ cup sugar gradually and beat until stiff but not dry; set aside. Cream butter, the remaining ¾ cup sugar and vanilla until fluffy. Stir in flour mixture alternately with milk until smooth and well blended. Fold in egg-white mixture gently but thoroughly. Divide batter between 2 greased and floured 8-inch layer-cake pans. Bake in preheated 350°F. oven 20 to 25 minutes or until golden brown and pick inserted in center comes out clean. Cool pans on racks 5 minutes, then invert on racks, turning layers top side up. Cool thoroughly. To assemble cake, spread about 1¼ cups frosting between layers. Spread remaining frosting on top and sides of cake, making deep swirls with small spatula. Decorate center with cherries and pineapple; surround with nut halves. **NOTE:** Cake can be assembled and stored in cake keeper in cool place up to 3 days before serving.

SCANDINAVIAN STRAWBERRY LAYER CAKE

2 eggs
¼ cup granulated sugar
½ cup farina (not quick)

1 quart strawberries, sliced and
  sweetened to taste (reserve a
  few whole berries for garnish)
Confectioners' sugar
Whipped cream (optional)

In small bowl of electric mixer beat eggs slightly; add granulated sugar and continue to beat until mixture is lemon-colored, light and fluffy. Stir in farina until well blended. Divide batter among 3 well-greased 8-inch layer-cake pans (layers will be thin). Bake in preheated 425°F. oven 10 minutes or until layers are golden brown and pull away from sides of pans. Invert on cake racks to cool (layers will become crisp). Just before serving, stack layers with strawberries; sprinkle top layer with confectioners' sugar and garnish with whole berries. To serve, cut in wedges and top with whipped cream. Serves 6.

MERINGUE CAKE SUPREME

Not a layer cake, exactly, but an equally beautiful
layered concoction just right for any special occasion.

4 egg whites	1 pint fresh strawberries
¼ teaspoon cream of tartar	2½ cups heavy cream
1¼ cups sugar (divided)	1 cup chopped walnuts
¼ teaspoon almond extract	

Beat egg whites with cream of tartar until almost stiff. Add 1 cup sugar a little at a time, beating constantly. Then add almond extract. When very stiff, spread on four 8-inch circles of brown paper to make meringue layers. Preheat oven to 400°F., put meringue layers in oven and turn off heat at once. Don't peek; let them stay in oven 2 hours. Remove from paper with spatula and turn out on cooling racks. If you break one, don't worry. It will be covered with filling and whipped-cream icing and won't show. To make filling, wash berries and set aside a few whole ones for decoration. Slice remainder (do not sweeten). Whip 1½ cups cream with remaining sugar until stiff. Fold in sliced strawberries and walnuts. Using platter or plate that cake will be served on, start with meringue layer, then one third of filling, another meringue layer, filling, meringue layer, filling, and top with meringue layer. Whip remaining cream for icing. Ice top and sides and refrigerate at least 4 hours but no longer than 6. Decorate with reserved whole berries. Cut with cake breaker and serve at the table. It's very rich, so small servings will serve 12.

MAPLE LAYER CAKE WITH SEA-FOAM FROSTING

The perfect cake to bake when the maple sap is
running and you can splurge on fresh syrup. For added
flavor, decorate cake with walnut halves.

½ cup butter or margarine, softened	3 teaspoons baking powder
¼ cup sugar	½ teaspoon each, baking soda and salt
2 eggs	¼ teaspoon ginger
1 cup maple syrup	1 teaspoon vanilla
2¼ cups unsifted all-purpose flour	Sea-foam Frosting (page 142)

Cream butter and sugar until light and fluffy. Add eggs, one at a time, beating thoroughly after each. Gradually beat in syrup. Add sifted dry ingredients alternately with ½ cup hot water, beating until smooth. Add vanilla and put in two 9-inch layer-cake pans lined on the bottom with waxed paper. Bake in moderate oven (350°F.) about 25 minutes. Let stand on cake racks about 5 minutes, then turn out and peel off paper. Turn right side up and cool thoroughly. Spread frosting between layers and on top and sides of cake.

STRAWBERRY-GLAZED LAYER CAKE

This is a one-layer cake topped with glistening fresh berries and cream.

⅓ cup butter or margarine, softened	1 teaspoon baking powder
Sugar	Salt
1 egg	⅓ cup milk
½ teaspoon vanilla	3 cups fresh strawberries, hulled
1¼ cups sifted cake flour	1 tablespoon cornstarch
	1 cup heavy cream

Cream butter and ⅔ cup sugar until well blended. Add egg and vanilla and beat until fluffy. Sift next 2 ingredients and ½ teaspoon salt together and add with milk to first mixture, beating until smooth. Spread in floured greased 8-inch layer-cake pan and bake in preheated 350°F. oven about 25 minutes. Cool in pan on cake rack, then turn out on serving plate and turn right side up. Put ¼ cup sugar, dash of salt and berries in heavy saucepan and heat, stirring gently, until sugar is dissolved and juice begins to drain from berries. Remove berries with spoon and arrange on cake. Blend 2 tablespoons berry juice with cornstarch. Add to remaining juice and cook, stirring, until clear and slightly thickened. Cool slightly, then spoon on cake. Chill until glaze is set. Just before serving, whip cream with ¼ cup sugar until stiff. Spread some on sides of cake. Using a pastry tube, pipe remaining cream around top edge of cake.

3
SMALL LOAF CAKES

A simple slice of loaf cake is a satisfying dessert. For something more elaborate, loaf cakes can be frosted before slicing, and of course can be embellished further by serving with ice cream or sauce. These loaf cakes may be small in size compared with other cakes, but they go a long way; the cakes are dense, and slices can be thin.

There is something here for every taste—Two-Way Pound Cakes and Orange-Glazed Gold Cake (both ideal as a base for fresh fruits, homemade ice cream or custard sauces), Chocolate-Nut Loaves, Carrot-Orange Loaf, Banana Loaf, Honey-Almond and more. Since the small loaf is a popular form for fruitcakes, two excellent holiday recipes have been included—one a light version, the other dark.

BANANA LOAF CAKE

½ cup butter or margarine, softened
¾ cup light-brown sugar, lightly packed
¾ cup granulated sugar
1 teaspoon vanilla
1 egg
1 egg yolk

1 cup mashed, very ripe banana
2 cups all-purpose flour
1 teaspoon baking powder
½ teaspoon each, baking soda and salt
¾ cup buttermilk
Lemon Confectioners' Sugar Frosting (page 144), optional

Cream butter. Gradually add sugars and beat until fluffy. Add vanilla, egg and yolk and beat well. Blend in banana, then add mixed dry ingredients alternately with buttermilk, beating after each addition until smooth. Pour into well-greased 9 x 5 x 3-inch loaf pan and bake in slow oven (325°F.) 55 minutes or until done. Cool in pan on cake rack 10 minutes. Turn out. Frost if desired.

TWO-WAY POUND CAKES

Any 2 variations (below)
1 cup butter or margarine,
   softened
2 cups sugar
½ teaspoon salt
1½ teaspoons vanilla

4 eggs
2¾ cups flour
½ teaspoon baking powder
½ teaspoon baking soda
1 cup buttermilk

Prepare ingredients for variations and set aside. In large bowl of mixer cream butter, sugar, salt and vanilla until fluffy. Add eggs, one at a time, and beat until well blended. Stir together flour, baking powder and baking soda. Stir into butter mixture alternately with buttermilk. Divide batter in half (about 3½ cups each) and stir one variation into each half. Turn into 2 greased and floured 9 x 5 x 3-inch loaf pans. Bake in preheated 325°F. oven 50 to 60 minutes or until pick inserted in center comes out clean. Cool in pans on racks 10 minutes, then turn cakes out on racks to cool completely, top side up. Wrap airtight and store in cool place up to 1 week or freeze up to 3 months. Makes 2 loaf cakes.
NOTE: Give on board or platter, wrapped in plastic and decorated with ribbon, in airtight decorated container or in foil topped with bow.

VARIATIONS: Add the following ingredients, as specified, for each variation.
COCONUT POUND CAKE ½ cup flaked coconut. Coconut Frosting (optional, page 145).
LEMONY CURRANT POUND CAKE ½ cup dried currants, 2 tablespoons lemon juice and 1 teaspoon grated lemon peel.
NUTMEG POUND CAKE 1 teaspoon ground nutmeg.
LIGHT SPICE POUND CAKE 1 teaspoon each ground cardamom, cinnamon, cloves and ginger.

BASIC LOAF CAKE

Extra moist with the addition of applesauce. Glaze basic loaf with Orange Glaze III, page 152, if desired.

2 cups flour
1 teaspoon baking soda
½ teaspoon baking powder
½ teaspoon salt
1 teaspoon cinnamon
½ teaspoon nutmeg
¼ teaspoon each, cloves and
   allspice

½ cup butter or margarine,
   softened
1 cup packed light-brown sugar
1 egg, at room temperature
1¼ cups applesauce, at room
   temperature
½ cup each, raisins and chopped
   walnuts

Mix well flour, baking soda, baking powder, salt and spices; set aside. Cream well butter and sugar. Add egg; beat until fluffy. Stir in flour mixture and applesauce. Stir in raisins and nuts. Turn into greased and lightly floured 9 x 5 x 3-inch loaf pan. Bake in preheated 350°F. oven 70 minutes or until pick inserted in center comes out clean. Cool in pan on rack 5 minutes. Remove from pan; cool completely. Serve plain or frost as desired.

VARIATIONS:
LEMON-GLAZED DIAMONDS Prepare Basic Loaf Cake as above. Turn batter into greased and floured 13 x 9 x 2-inch pan. Bake in preheated 375°F. oven 25 minutes or until pick inserted in center comes out clean. Drizzle with Lemon Glaze (page 152) while warm. Cool; cut in 24 diamonds.
AFTER-SCHOOL TINY CUPCAKES Prepare Basic Loaf Cake as above. Drop rounded measuring-tablespoonfuls of batter into greased 2½-inch cupcake pans. Bake in preheated 375°F. oven 15 minutes or until pick inserted in center comes out clean. Remove from pan to rack; cool. Makes 36.
DESSERT SQUARES Prepare Basic Loaf Cake as above. Turn batter into greased and floured 9-inch square pan. Bake in preheated 350°F. oven about 35 minutes or until pick inserted in center comes out clean. Cut in squares. Serve warm with Lemon Cream I (page 148). Makes 6 large servings.

EASY DARK FRUITCAKES

1 box (1 pound) brown sugar	2 teaspoons cinnamon
1 pound (2½ cups) mixed chopped candied fruit	1 teaspoon salt
1 package (15 ounces) raisins	¼ teaspoon ground cloves
1½ cups orange juice	3 cups flour
2 tablespoons cocoa powder	1 teaspoon baking soda
2 tablespoons rum or brandy	1 cup chopped walnuts
2 tablespoons butter or margarine	Orange Glaze II (optional, page 152)
	Candied fruit (optional)

In heavy saucepan combine sugar, fruit, raisins, orange juice, cocoa, rum, butter, cinnamon, salt and cloves. Bring to boil and boil, stirring occasionally, 5 minutes. Cool completely. Stir together flour, baking soda and walnuts. Stir into fruit mixture until well blended. Turn into 3 well-greased and floured 8 x 4-inch loaf pans. Bake in preheated 325°F. oven 1 hour or until pick inserted in center comes out clean. Remove from pan. Cool completely. Wrap in cheesecloth soaked in brandy or sherry, then wrap in foil. Store in refrigerator. If desired, cheesecloth may be resoaked as it becomes dry. Cakes will keep 2 months. Before giving, drizzle with Orange Glaze II and decorate with candied fruit.

LIGHT CANDIED FRUITCAKE

Make 4 to 6 weeks ahead to allow for aging and increased flavor.

1 cup each:
 Coarsely chopped pitted
  prunes or dates
 Golden raisins
 Diced candied pineapple
 Minced candied orange peel
 Thinly sliced candied
  cherries
 Chopped almonds or
  pecans
2½ cups flour, divided
2 teaspoons baking powder

1½ teaspoons salt
1 tablespoon cinnamon
1 teaspoon allspice
½ teaspoon cloves
1½ cups sugar
1¼ cups shortening
6 eggs
½ cup pineapple or other fruit
 juice
Candied-cherry halves and/or
 whole almonds for decoration
Brandy (optional)

Mix fruits and chopped almonds with 1 cup flour. Stir together remaining 1½ cups flour, baking powder, salt, cinnamon, allspice and cloves; set aside. Cream sugar and shortening, beating until light. Add eggs, one at a time, beating well after each. Add flour mixture alternately with fruit juice. Pour over fruit-nut mixture and mix well. Pack batter lightly in three 8 x 4 x 2-inch loaf pans lined on bottom with waxed paper. Decorate with cherry halves. Bake in preheated 250°F. oven about 3 hours or until cake is firm and pick inserted in center comes out clean. (Place shallow pan of water on bottom rack of oven while cake is baking.) Loosen edges of cake; let stand 20 minutes, then remove from pan. Wrap in cheesecloth soaked in brandy, then wrap in foil. Store in refrigerator. If desired, cheesecloth may be resoaked in brandy as it becomes dry. Will keep 2 months.

COFFEE-RAISIN SPICE CAKE

1 cup coffee
1 cup granulated sugar or packed
 brown sugar (best with brown)
1½ cups raisins, chopped
⅓ cup butter, margarine or other
 shortening
½ teaspoon ground cloves
1 teaspoon cinnamon

1 teaspoon nutmeg
½ teaspoon salt
½ teaspoon baking powder
1 teaspoon baking soda
2 cups all-purpose flour
Lemon Confectioners' Sugar
 Frosting (optional, page 144)

Put first 7 ingredients in saucepan, bring to boil and boil 3 minutes; cool thoroughly. Add remaining ingredients, except frosting, and mix well. Put in 9 x 5 x 3-inch loaf pan lined on bottom with waxed paper and bake in slow oven (275°F.) 1 hour and 10 minutes or until done. Turn out on rack and peel off paper. Turn right side up. Serve plain or top with thin frosting.

CARROT-ORANGE LOAF

2 cups flour
1 teaspoon each, baking powder
   and baking soda
½ teaspoon salt
½ teaspoon each, allspice and
   nutmeg
Grated peel of 1 orange

2 large carrots, grated (1 cup)
½ cup butter or margarine,
   softened
1 cup packed brown sugar
2 eggs
1 cup walnuts, chopped fine

Stir together flour, baking powder, baking soda, salt, allspice and nutmeg; set aside. Combine orange peel and carrots; set aside. In large bowl cream butter. Gradually beat in sugar until light and fluffy. Beat in eggs, one at a time, until well blended. Alternately stir in flour mixture and carrot mixture until well blended. Stir in walnuts. Turn into greased 9 x 5 x 3-inch loaf pan. Bake in preheated 325°F. oven 50 to 60 minutes or until pick inserted in center comes out clean. Cool in pan 5 minutes; turn out to cool completely.

HONEY-ALMOND CAKE

2 cups flour
3 teaspoons baking powder
½ teaspoon salt
½ cup butter or margarine,
   softened
½ cup sugar

2 eggs
½ cup honey
¾ cup milk
½ cup blanched chopped
   almonds
2 tablespoons sliced almonds for
   garnish (optional)

Mix well flour, baking powder and salt; set aside. In large bowl of mixer cream butter and sugar until light. Beat in eggs until fluffy. With mixer at high speed gradually add honey in thin stream; beat until light. Stir in flour mixture alternately with milk. Stir in chopped almonds. Turn into well-greased 9 x 5 x 3-inch loaf pan. Sprinkle with sliced almonds. Bake in preheated 350°F. oven 50 to 60 minutes or until pick inserted in center comes out clean. Cool in pan 10 minutes. Turn out on rack. Cool completely. Wrap airtight. Keeps about 1 week. **NOTE:** Sliced almonds absorb moisture from cake and become translucent during storage.

ORANGE-GLAZED GOLD CAKE

*With or without the glaze, this is a versatile, basic
and delicious loaf cake.*

2¼ cups sifted cake flour
1 cup sugar
2 teaspoons baking powder
1 teaspoon salt
¼ cup margarine, softened

¼ cup vegetable shortening
1 teaspoon vanilla
5 egg yolks, unbeaten
¾ cup milk
Orange Glaze I (page 152)

Sift first 4 ingredients into large bowl of electric mixer. Add next 4 ingredients and ½ cup milk. Blend ingredients and beat 2 minutes at medium speed or 300 vigorous strokes by hand, scraping sides and bottom of bowl several times. Add remaining milk and beat 2 minutes longer. Put batter in 9 x 5 x 3-inch loaf pan lined on bottom with waxed paper. Bake in moderate oven (350°F.) 1 hour, or until done. Remove from oven and, leaving cake in pan, punch holes with wooden skewer. Spoon glaze slowly on cake so that mixture runs into holes. When cake is slightly firm, turn out of pan and turn right side up on rack. Cool. **NOTE:** You can substitute ½ cup butter for the margarine and vegetable shortening called for.

CHOCOLATE-NUT LOAVES

*A rich, delicious brownielike cake, ideal with vanilla
or coffee ice cream.*

2½ cups sifted cake flour
1 teaspoon baking soda
1 teaspoon salt
1 cup butter or margarine,
   softened
2 cups sugar
5 eggs

3 squares unsweetened
   chocolate, melted and cooled
1 cup buttermilk
2 teaspoons vanilla
1 cup finely chopped nuts
Chocolate Glaze I (page 151)
Pistachio nuts

Sift flour with baking soda and salt. Cream butter. Gradually add sugar, creaming well after each addition. Add eggs, one at a time, beating thoroughly after each. Blend in chocolate. Add flour mixture alternately with buttermilk, a small amount at a time, beating after each addition until smooth. Add vanilla and nuts and mix well. Pour into two 9 x 5 x 3-inch loaf pans lined on bottoms with waxed paper. Bake in moderate oven (350°F.) 60 minutes or until done. Cool on cake racks 10 minutes, then remove from pans, peel off paper and turn right side up. Cool on racks. Pour warm glaze on cakes and spread with spatula. Before glaze hardens, sprinkle cakes generously around sides and edges with nuts. When firm, wrap and store airtight.

4
LARGE LOAF CAKES

Whether baked in rectangular, square or round pans, single-layer, large loaf cakes are the perfect dessert for big informal gatherings—community events, large family picnics, school meetings or reunions—you name it. That they are economical crowd-pleasers should not put a limit on their appeal—large loaf cakes can be baked up for a few friends and small families, too. They are the perfect ending to a comfortable evening meal at home.

One of the distinctions of this type of cake is the versatility of ingredients— from apples, pears and peaches to pumpkins and zucchini—no-nonsense, healthful blends of fruits, nuts, spices. This is a big category of popular cakes, and it's easy to see why, with so many marvelous offerings in *Woman's Day*: Old-Time Apple Cake, extramoist Tropical Carrot Cake; Zucchini Cake, with its tangy Orange Icing; Easy Almond Cake; rich, flavorful Chocolate-Buttermilk Cake with Chocolate Glaze—they are all here, the very best of the large loaf cakes.

EASY ALMOND CAKE

1 cup flour	¼ teaspoon salt
½ teaspoon baking soda	2 eggs
¼ cup margarine, softened	½ cup buttermilk or yogurt
1 cup sugar	2 tablespoons sliced almonds or
1 teaspoon almond extract	finely chopped nuts

Stir together flour and baking soda; set aside. In large bowl of mixer beat margarine, sugar, almond extract, salt and eggs until light and lemon-colored. Alternately stir in buttermilk and flour mixture until well blended. Turn into greased 9-inch layer-cake or 8 x 8 x 2-inch pan. Sprinkle top with almonds. Bake in preheated 350°F. oven 25 to 30 minutes or until pick inserted in center comes out clean. Cool on rack. Cut in wedges or rectangles. If desired, serve topped with sweetened sliced fresh or thawed frozen strawberries and vanilla ice cream. Serves 8.

CHOCOLATE-BUTTERMILK CAKE WITH CHOCOLATE GLAZE

1¼ cups flour
½ teaspoon baking soda
½ cup butter or margarine, softened
1 cup sugar
1 teaspoon vanilla
½ teaspoon salt

3 eggs
2 squares (2 ounces) unsweetened chocolate, melted and cooled
½ cup chopped nuts
½ cup buttermilk
Chocolate Glaze I (page 151)

Mix flour with baking soda; set aside. Cream butter, sugar, vanilla and salt until fluffy. Beat in eggs, one at a time, until well blended. Stir in chocolate and nuts. Stir in flour mixture alternately with buttermilk until smooth and well blended. Pour into greased and floured 9 x 9 x 2-inch baking pan. Bake in preheated 350°F. oven 35 minutes or until pick inserted in center comes out clean. Cool on rack. Pour warm Chocolate Glaze I on cake, then spread with spatula and let set. Serves 8 to 10.

PUMPKIN SPICE CAKE

2¼ cups sifted cake flour
1 tablespoon baking powder
¼ teaspoon baking soda
½ teaspoon salt
1 teaspoon cinnamon
¼ teaspoon ground ginger
½ cup granulated sugar
½ cup margarine, at room temperature

1 cup packed light-brown sugar
¾ cup canned pumpkin
½ cup buttermilk
1 egg
2 egg yolks
Creamy Molasses Frosting (page 146)

Sift first 7 ingredients. Put margarine in large bowl of electric mixer (or other mixing bowl if mixer is not available) and stir just to soften. Add flour mixture, brown sugar, pumpkin and ¼ cup buttermilk. Beat 2 minutes at low speed of mixer or 300 vigorous strokes by hand. Add remaining buttermilk and next 2 ingredients and beat 1 minute longer or 150 strokes by hand. Pour into greased and floured 13 x 9 x 2-inch pan. Bake in moderate oven (350°F.) 45 minutes or until done. Cool in pan; spread with frosting.

CARROT-APPLESAUCE CAKE

Applesauce makes popular carrot cake moister and more delicious. Good for making ahead and long keeping. Cake may be baked in a variety of sizes and shapes. Chopped nuts make a flavorful decorative topping, eliminate frosting.

2¾ cups flour
3 teaspoons baking soda
1 teaspoon salt
3 teaspoons cinnamon
1 teaspoon nutmeg
4 eggs
¾ cup oil
2 cups sugar
1 teaspoon vanilla

1 jar (15 ounces) applesauce
  (about 1⅔ cups)
3 cups shredded carrots (about 1
  pound)
1 cup golden raisins
1 cup chopped walnuts, divided
Cream-cheese Frosting I
  (page 145), optional

In large bowl mix flour, baking soda, salt, cinnamon and nutmeg; set aside. With whisk, beat eggs. Stir in oil, sugar and vanilla. Add applesauce and carrots; mix well. Add to flour mixture, stirring just to moisten. Fold in raisins and ½ cup walnuts. Pour into greased pan or pans (see specifics below). Sprinkle with remaining ½ cup walnuts. (Exception: For fluted tube cake sprinkle nuts in *bottom* of heavily greased 12-cup pan *before* adding batter.) Bake in preheated 350°F. oven as specified below or until pick inserted in center comes out clean. For all cakes *except tube cake:* Cool in pan on rack. *Tube cake:* Cool in pan on rack 15 minutes, then invert on rack; cool thoroughly. Store in airtight container or cake keeper. Will keep well 4 to 5 days.

Cake may be baked in any one of the following ways:

• One *heavily greased* 12-cup fluted tube pan (with nuts sprinkled in bottom). Bake about 65 minutes.
• One 13 x 9 x 2-inch baking pan or 12 x 9 x 1 ½-inch foil lasagna pan. Bake about 45 minutes.
• Six 6 x 3-inch small foil loaf pans. Bake 40 to 45 minutes.
• Four 8 x 6-inch rectangular foil pans. Bake 35 to 40 minutes.
• Three 8 x 4 x 2½-inch foil loaf pans. Bake 45 to 50 minutes.
• Two 8- or 9-inch square baking pans. Bake 35 to 40 minutes.
• About thirty-six 2½-inch cupcakes. Bake 20 to 25 minutes.

OLD-TIME APPLE CAKE

A moist, nutritious cake low in fat and calories.

1 cup sugar
3 medium apples, peeled and
    diced (about 2 cups)
1 egg, slightly beaten

1 cup flour
1 teaspoon each, baking soda and
    cinnamon
4 tablespoons wheat germ,
    divided

In large bowl sprinkle sugar over apples; let stand about 30 minutes or until juicy. Stir in egg, flour, baking soda, cinnamon and 3 tablespoons wheat germ until well blended. Turn into greased 8-inch square baking pan; sprinkle with remaining 1 tablespoon wheat germ. Bake in 375°F. oven 30 minutes or until pick inserted in center comes out clean. Cool on rack; serve warm or at room temperature. Store leftovers in covered pan at room temperature. Serves 8.

TROPICAL CARROT CAKE

Slices best after standing several hours.

2 cups flour
2 teaspoons baking powder
1 teaspoon each, baking soda and
    cinnamon
½ teaspoon each, salt, nutmeg
    and allspice
4 eggs
2 cups sugar
1¼ cups oil
2 cups finely shredded raw
    carrots (about 6 medium)

1 can (about 8 ounces) crushed
    pineapple, drained (about ¾
    cup)
1 cup chopped walnuts
½ cup flaked coconut
Tropical Butter Frosting (page
    144) or Cream-cheese Frosting
    II (page 146)
Shredded orange peel (optional)
Confectioners' sugar (optional)

Stir together flour, baking powder, baking soda, cinnamon, salt, nutmeg and allspice; set aside. In large bowl of mixer beat eggs slightly. Gradually beat in sugar until mixture is thick and lemon-colored. With rubber spatula gradually stir in oil. Add flour mixture, carrots, pineapple, walnuts and coconut; stir until well mixed. Divide among 3 greased, floured 9-inch layer pans or turn into greased, floured 13 x 9 x 2-inch pan. Bake in preheated 350°F. oven 40 minutes for layers, 55 to 60 minutes for sheet cake, or until pick inserted in center comes out clean. **LAYERS** Cool in pans 10 minutes, then turn out on racks to cool. Fill and frost top of cake with preferred frosting. Garnish with shredded orange peel. **SHEET CAKE** Cool in pan on rack. Frost in pan or sprinkle with confectioners' sugar. Serves 16.

CINNAMON-RHUBARB CAKE

Best made 12 to 24 hours ahead for flavor development.

2 cups flour
1 teaspoon baking powder
½ teaspoon each, baking soda and salt
1¼ teaspoons ground cinnamon, divided
½ cup butter or margarine, softened

2 cups packed dark-brown sugar, divided
1 egg
1 teaspoon vanilla
1 cup buttermilk
2 cups finely diced fresh rhubarb
⅔ cup chopped walnuts
Heavy cream, whipped to soft peaks

Stir together flour, baking powder, baking soda, salt and ¼ teaspoon cinnamon; set aside. In large bowl of mixer beat butter and 1½ cups sugar until creamed. Add egg and vanilla and beat until fluffy. Add flour mixture alternately with buttermilk, beginning and ending with flour mixture and beating after each addition. Stir in rhubarb and nuts. Spread smooth in greased 9 x 13 x 2-inch pan. Mix remaining ½ cup sugar with remaining 1 teaspoon cinnamon and sprinkle on batter. Bake in preheated 350°F. oven 45 minutes or until pick inserted in center comes out clean. Cool in pan on rack. Cake is best if stored 12 to 24 hours before serving; wrap airtight. Cut in bars and serve at room temperature. Or reheat, cut in squares and serve topped with whipped cream. Serves 12 to 15.

CRANBERRY SPICE CAKE

½ cup butter or margarine
1 cup sugar
1 egg
1 cup golden raisins
½ cup chopped walnuts or other nuts
1½ cups all-purpose flour
¼ teaspoon salt

1 teaspoon baking soda
1 teaspoon baking powder
1 teaspoon cinnamon
½ teaspoon ground cloves
1 can (1 pound) whole-cranberry sauce
Cranberry and Cream-cheese Frosting (page 145)

Cream butter and sugar. Add egg and beat well. Stir in raisins and nuts. Mix dry ingredients and stir into first mixture. Reserve ¼ cup cranberry sauce for frosting and stir remainder into mixture. Spread in greased 13 x 9 x 2-inch pan and bake in moderate oven (350°F.) 40 minutes or until done. Cool in pan on rack; spread with frosting.

SPICY PEAR UPSIDE-DOWN CAKE

4 pears, peeled, cored and sliced
⅓ cup sugar mixed with 1 tablespoon flour and ¼ teaspoon each cinnamon and nutmeg
3 tablespoons butter or margarine
½ cup sugar

1 egg
½ cup buttermilk
1 cup flour
½ teaspoon each, baking powder and vanilla
¼ teaspoon each, baking soda, salt, cloves, ginger and nutmeg
Topping

In greased 8 x 8 x 2-inch baking pan mix pears and sugar mixture, then smooth in even layer; set aside. To make batter, cream butter and sugar until fluffy; beat in egg and buttermilk, then flour, baking powder, vanilla, baking soda, salt, cloves, ginger and nutmeg. Pour over pear mixture, sprinkle with Topping and bake in preheated 350°F. oven 30 to 35 minutes or until pick inserted in *cake layer* comes out clean and pears are tender. Cool slightly. Cut in squares and serve warm. Serves 8.

TOPPING With pastry blender or fork cut 2 tablespoons softened butter or margarine into ¼ cup flour and ¼ cup packed brown sugar until mixture is crumbly.

ZUCCHINI CAKE

Bumper crops of zucchini have helped promote this cake. Its spicy overtones are complemented by tangy Orange Icing. If cake is to be wrapped, arrange nut halves or sprinkle chopped nuts on icing to keep it from sticking to wrapping. This medium-size recipe can be baked in various shapes and sizes.

2½ cups flour
2 teaspoons baking powder
1 teaspoon baking soda
1 teaspoon salt
2 teaspoons cinnamon
½ teaspoon cloves
3 eggs

½ cup oil
1⅓ cups sugar
½ cup orange juice
1 teaspoon almond extract
1½ cups shredded zucchini (about 2 medium-size)
Orange Icing (page 144)

In large bowl mix flour, baking powder, baking soda, salt, cinnamon and cloves; set aside. With whisk, beat eggs. Stir in oil, sugar, juice, extract and zucchini; mix well. Add to flour mixture, stirring just to moisten. Pour into greased pan or pans (see specifics below). Bake in preheated 350°F. oven as specified below or until pick inserted in center comes out clean. For all cakes *except tube cake:* Cool in pan on rack. *Tube cake:* Cool in pan on rack 15 minutes, then invert on rack to cool thoroughly. Store in airtight container or keeper. Will keep well 4 to 5 days. When you plan to serve, spread with Orange Icing. (If icing is too thick to flow well on tube cake, thin with a little orange juice.) If desired, decorate icing with nut halves or sprinkle with chopped nuts.

Cake may be baked in any one of the following ways:
• One *heavily greased* 10-cup fluted tube pan. Bake 55 to 60 minutes.
• One 13 x 9 x 2-inch baking pan or 12 x 9 x 1½-inch foil lasagna pan. Bake 35 to 40 minutes.
• Four 6 x 3-inch small foil loaf pans. Bake about 40 minutes.
• Two 8 x 4 x 2½-inch foil loaf pans. Bake 40 to 45 minutes.
• Two 8- or 9-inch square baking pans. Bake about 35 minutes.
• Two 8 x 6-inch rectangular foil pans. Bake about 35 minutes.
• About twenty-four 2½-inch cupcakes. Bake 20 to 25 minutes.

SPICY PRUNE CAKE

Prunes have a high iron and vitamin content and give quick energy as snacks. For calorie counters, ¼ pound of prunes has about 268 calories. But that's before you add them to this superb cake. For variation, substitute apricots for prunes.

1 cup quick-cooking rolled oats	1 egg
1 cup (after pitting) cut-up dried prunes	1½ cups flour
	1 teaspoon baking soda
1¼ cups boiling water	¾ teaspoon salt
½ cup butter or margarine	1 teaspoon cinnamon
½ cup granulated sugar	¼ teaspoon ground cloves
1 cup packed brown sugar	Vanilla Frosting (page 146)

Put oats and prunes in bowl and cover with the boiling water. Stir well, cover and let stand 20 minutes. Cream butter; gradually add sugars, beating until fluffy. Add egg and oat mixture and mix well. Stir in sifted dry ingredients. Pour into greased 9-inch square pan and bake in preheated 350°F. oven 45 to 50 minutes. Cool in pan, then spread with frosting. When firm, cut cake in squares.

BLUEBERRY CRUMB CAKE

½ cup butter or margarine
½ cup sugar
1 egg
2 cups all-purpose flour
¼ teaspoon salt
1 tablespoon baking powder

⅔ cup milk
2 cups blueberries
1 tablespoon lemon juice
Topping

Cream butter, add sugar and beat until creamy. Add egg and beat until light. Combine flour, salt and baking powder. Add to first mixture alternately with milk. Put in greased 13 x 9 x 2-inch pan. Sprinkle dough with blueberries mixed with lemon juice. Then sprinkle with topping. Bake in moderate oven (350°F.) about 50 minutes. Serve warm.

TOPPING Mix ⅓ cup each, sugar and flour, and ½ teaspoon cinnamon. Mix in ¼ cup butter or margarine until crumbly.

FRUITCAKE LAYERED WITH ALMOND PASTE

A rich, dense cake with thin layers of almond paste.
Improves with age. Ships well.

1 cup finely chopped mixed
    candied fruits
½ cup currants
¼ cup brandy or light rum
1 can (8 ounces) or 1 package (7
    ounces) almond paste, cut in
    half

1½ cups butter or margarine,
    softened
1 cup granulated sugar
6 eggs
3½ cups flour
Confectioners' sugar

At least 1 day before baking cake, combine candied fruits, currants and brandy in covered container; marinate at least 24 hours. Shape each piece almond paste to a square. Roll out each to 9-inch square on pastry cloth lightly sprinkled with confectioners' sugar; set aside. Grease a 9-inch square baking pan; line bottom with waxed paper; grease again; set aside. In large bowl, cream butter; gradually add sugar; cream until light and fluffy. Add eggs, one at a time, beating well after each. Stir in flour alternately with marinated fruits. (Most liquid should be absorbed; if not, do not add more than 2 tablespoons.) Spread enough batter (about 1 cup) in prepared pan to cover bottom. Top with 1 square almond paste. Spread half the remaining batter over almond paste; top with remaining square almond paste. Cover with remaining batter. Bake in preheated 350° F. oven 1 hour or until golden brown and pick inserted in center comes out clean. Cool in pan on rack 10 minutes. Unmold; peel off waxed paper. Turn top side up; cool completely before wrapping airtight. Can be refrigerated up to six weeks. Before serving, dust with confectioners' sugar. Cut in quarters, then ¼-inch-thick slices. Serves 72.

OATMEAL CAKE WITH BROILED TOPPING

1½ cups flour
1 teaspoon baking soda
¾ teaspoon cinnamon
½ teaspoon salt
1 cup rolled oats (any kind)
1¼ cups boiling water

½ cup margarine, softened
½ cup each, packed light-brown
  sugar and granulated sugar
2 eggs
1 teaspoon vanilla
Broiled Topping (page 153)

Combine flour, baking soda, cinnamon and salt; set aside. Combine oats and water; let stand 20 minutes. In bowl beat margarine, sugars, eggs and vanilla until light in color. Stir in oat mixture, then flour mixture. Pour into greased and floured 9-inch square pan and bake in preheated 350°F. oven 50 minutes or until pick inserted in center comes out clean. Spread with Broiled Topping and broil 5 minutes or until bubbly. Serve warm or at room temperature.

SPICY SOUTHERN GINGERBREAD

For an upside-down cake, put 1 pound peeled, sliced and sweetened peaches under the batter before baking.

2 eggs
¾ cup packed brown sugar
¾ cup light molasses
¾ cup butter, melted
2½ cups all-purpose flour
2 teaspoons baking powder

2 teaspoons ginger
1½ teaspoons cinnamon
½ teaspoon each, cloves,
  nutmeg, baking soda and salt
Whipped cream

Beat first 4 ingredients together. Mix together dry ingredients and add with 1 cup boiling water to first mixture. Beat well, then pour into well-greased 13 x 9 x 2-inch baking pan. Bake in preheated 350°F. oven about 35 minutes. Serve with whipped cream.

FLAMBÉED YOGURT CAKE

(color plate 7, top)
A spectacular dessert winner of the Woman's Day
Silver Spoon Award, *submitted by Mindy Butalia. It
might be stretching things to call this a "round loaf
cake" but it is so delicious it had to be included here.
An easily mixed yogurt cake is cut in wedges, soaked
in an apricot nectar sauce, transferred to a chafing
dish and flamed at the table. Warm the cake, sauce
and rum before flaming, and turn down the dining
room lights for a full dramatic effect.*

2 eggs
1¼ cups plus ¼ teaspoon sugar,
  divided
½ cup flour
½ teaspoon baking powder
½ cup plain yogurt
½ teaspoon vanilla and/or grated
  lemon peel

1 can (12 ounces) apricot nectar
  (1½ cups)
¼ cup water
Candied red cherries and green
  pineapple for garnish
¼ cup rum

In small bowl beat eggs and ½ cup sugar 7 to 10 minutes or until sugar dissolves and mixture is light and fluffy. Mix well flour and baking powder. Mix well yogurt and vanilla. Alternately add flour mixture and yogurt mixture to egg mixture, beating well after each addition. Pour into well-greased and floured 8-inch layer-cake pan. Bake in preheated 400°F. oven 20 to 25 minutes or until golden brown (cake may puff up). Meanwhile, in saucepan bring to boil ¾ cup sugar, the apricot nectar and water. Boil 5 minutes; cool. Remove cake from oven; cool slightly (cake may fall). Cut in 8 wedges; pour on apricot syrup. Gently loosen cake from pan to allow syrup to get underneath. Cover and let stand at room temperature overnight or refrigerate up to 3 days. To serve: Warm cake in preheated 325°F. oven 10 to 12 minutes; turn out on warmed serving dish. Garnish with cherries and pineapple. Sprinkle with remaining ¼ teaspoon sugar. Warm rum over low heat; pour over cake; ignite. Serve after flames die. Serves 8.

5
TUBE CAKES AND BUNDT CAKES

Baked in the traditional tube or bundt pans, these distinctive, ring-shaped cakes are imposing in appearance and make an outstanding dessert—enough, usually, to serve at least ten or twelve people.

Tube cakes include the classic angel or chiffon cakes—high, light and airy, using only egg whites and no shortening. The selection includes several of this type of cake, as well as extra rich pound cake, and cakes using fruits, baked in tube pans. Since most of the cakes in this chapter are tall, they lend themselves to eye-pleasing, imaginative preparation for serving. They are easy to split crossways into layers (see page 12) to be filled and frosted. They can also be hollowed out from the top, leaving a shell about an inch thick, and filled with custard, whipped cream or ice cream. About a quart of ice cream or custard or other filling is enough for a ten-inch cake. If you want to save the top of the cake for a frosting surface, cut a one-inch layer from the top of the cake before hollowing; replace it after filling. You can frost a filled cake, leave it plain or, where using an ice cream filling, freeze it until about twenty minutes before serving.

ORANGE CHIFFON CAKE

*Separate eggs while cold and let reach room
temperature before starting cake.*

2 cups unsifted all-purpose flour
1½ cups sugar
3 teaspoons baking powder
1 teaspoon salt
½ cup vegetable oil

7 egg yolks
2 tablespoons grated orange rind
1 cup egg whites (7 or 8)
½ teaspoon cream of tartar

In large bowl stir together first 4 ingredients. Make a well in center and add in order: oil, egg yolks, ¾ cup cold water and the orange rind. Stir until smooth. Put egg whites and cream of tartar in large mixing bowl. Beat with mixer or rotary beater until *very stiff* peaks are formed. Gradually pour egg-yolk mixture over beaten whites, folding gently *just* until blended. Pour into ungreased 10 x 4-inch tube pan. Bake in slow oven (325°F.) 65 to 75 minutes or until top springs back when touched lightly with finger. Invert pan on funnel and let hang until cake is completely cool. To remove from pan, loosen first by moving spatula up and down against side of pan. Next, hit edge of pan against counter top and then shake cake out. Leave cake bottom-side up and frost or decorate as desired.

ORANGE-LEMON CREAM CAKE

*This is an elegant tour de force—an impressive
creamy-textured cake similar to Zuppa Inglese. The
orange-lemon filling soaks into the cake overnight and
should be spooned back over the cake before frosting
with whipped cream.*

1 Orange Chiffon Cake (above)
¼ cup cornstarch
Sugar
Dash of salt
2 cups orange juice
⅓ cup lemon juice

Grated rind of 2 oranges (about 2
    tablespoons, orange part only)
4 eggs, separated
1½ cups heavy cream
Canned mandarin oranges,
    drained

Using sharp thin-bladed knife, slice cake in 5 crosswise layers. In top part of double boiler mix cornstarch, 1½ cups sugar and the salt. Add 1 cup water, fruit juices and rind. Mix well and put over boiling water. Cook, stirring frequently, at least 20 minutes. When thickened, pour gradually, stirring, over beaten egg yolks. Put back in double boiler and cook, stirring, about 5 minutes. Remove from heat. Beat egg whites until stiff and almost dry. Fold into mixture until well blended. Spread between layers and on top and sides of cake. (Each layer will take about 1¼ cups.) Chill overnight. When ready to serve, add sugar to taste to cream and whip until stiff. Spread on top and sides of cake. (If desired, reserve ¼ cup cream for whipped-cream rosettes.) Arrange mandarin-orange segments in flower designs on top of cake and, if desired, make rosette in center of each design with pastry tube. Serves 16.

GEORGIA PECAN CAKE

Golden raisins and baked-in brandy distinguish this light and aromatic cake.

3¾ cups flour
1 teaspoon baking powder
4 teaspoons nutmeg
4 cups chopped pecans (about 1 pound)
5 cups golden raisins

½ pound red candied cherries, quartered
1 cup butter or margarine, softened
2 cups sugar
6 eggs
½ cup brandy

Stir together flour, baking powder and nutmeg. Mix ½ cup flour mixture with pecans, raisins and cherries. In large bowl of electric mixer cream butter and sugar until fluffy. Add eggs, two at a time, beating thoroughly after each addition. At low speed add remaining flour mixture alternately with brandy, mixing after each until blended. Add pecan fruit mixture and mix thoroughly. Turn into greased 10-inch tube pan. Bake in center of preheated 275°F. oven about 3 hours. Cool pan on rack about 15 minutes, then invert on rack, turning cake topside up. Cool thoroughly.

STONEWALL JACKSON CAKE

A Southerner's delight.

¾ cup butter, softened
1 cup sugar
6 egg yolks
1½ cups all-purpose flour
1 teaspoon baking powder

⅛ teaspoon salt
2 tablespoons brandy or whiskey
5 egg whites
Chocolate Frosting I (page 143)
Walnut or pecan halves

Cream butter and sugar until light and fluffy. Add egg yolks, one at a time, beating thoroughly after each addition. Sift dry ingredients into bowl. Fold in first mixture. Add brandy and mix well. Beat egg whites until stiff and fold into mixture. Pour into greased and floured 10-inch tube pan. Preheat oven to 400°F. Put pan in oven and turn control to 325°F. Bake about 45 minutes. Let stand in pan 10 minutes, then turn out on rack to cool. Spread frosting on top and sides of cake and, while it is still soft, cover completely with nut halves to resemble a stone wall.

GREEK LEMON CAKE

*This feathery cake is lovely served with ice cream or
fresh fruit marinated in a liqueur.*

3 cups cake flour or 2¾ cups all-
purpose flour
1 teaspoon baking soda
¼ teaspoon salt
6 eggs, separated

2 cups sugar, divided
1 cup butter or margarine,
softened
2 teaspoons grated lemon peel
2 tablespoons lemon juice
1 cup plain yogurt

Stir together flour, baking soda and salt; set aside. In large bowl of mixer beat egg whites
until soft peaks form. Gradually add ½ cup sugar, beating until stiff but glossy peaks form;
set aside. Beat butter, remaining 1½ cups sugar, egg yolks, lemon peel and juice until
fluffy. Stir flour mixture alternately with yogurt into creamed butter mixture, then gently
fold into egg-white mixture. Pour into greased 10-inch plain or fluted tube pan. Bake in
preheated 350°F. oven 50 to 60 minutes or until pick inserted in center comes out clean.
Cool in pan 10 minutes, then turn out on rack to finish cooling. Serves 12.

CHOCOLATE-FROSTED MARBLE CAKE

*A tender, buttery white cake complemented by dark
chocolate cake and rich chocolaty frosting.*

4 squares semisweet chocolate
or 4 ounces (¾ cup) chocolate
pieces
1 cup butter, softened
2 cups sugar
8 egg whites (separate one at a
time, using 6 yolks for
frosting)

3¼ cups sifted cake flour
2 teaspoons baking powder
⅛ teaspoon salt
1 cup milk
2 teaspoons vanilla
Rich Chocolate Frosting (page
143)

Melt chocolate over hot water in top part of double boiler. Remove from water and cool.
With waxed paper, line bottom of 4-inch deep 10-inch tube pan. Cream butter in large
mixing bowl. Gradually add sugar and cream until light and fluffy. Add egg whites, one
or two at a time, beating well after each. Fold in sifted dry ingredients alternately with
mixture of milk and vanilla. beginning and ending with flour mixture. Add one third of
batter (about 2 cups) to melted chocolate and blend well. Pour half the remaining white
batter into lined pan. Spoon in chocolate batter and pour remaining white batter on top.
Run small spatula through batter several times to marbleize. With rack in center of oven,
bake in moderate oven (350°F.) 50 to 60 minutes. Cool on cake rack 10 minutes. Run
spatula around edges of cake and around tube. Turn out on rack, remove paper, cool and
turn top up. Spread with frosting, including center part. Make swirls with small spatula.

ORANGE-RAISIN-NUT CAKE

3 cups flour
1½ teaspoons each, baking
    powder and baking soda
¾ teaspoon salt
1 cup each, chopped raisins and
    nuts
¾ cup butter or margarine,
    softened

2 cups sugar, divided
3 eggs
Grated peel of 1 orange and 1
    lemon
1½ cups buttermilk
Juice of 1 orange and 1 lemon

Stir together flour, baking powder, baking soda, salt, raisins and nuts; set aside. In large bowl of mixer cream butter with 1½ cups sugar until fluffy. Beat in eggs, one at a time, until light and well blended. Stir in orange and lemon peels. Stir in flour mixture alternately with buttermilk until well blended. Pour into greased 3-quart fluted tube pan. Bake in preheated 350°F. oven 1 hour or until pick inserted in center comes out clean. Meanwhile mix remaining ½ cup sugar with orange and lemon juices until sugar is dissolved; set aside. Place cake in pan on rack. Prick with skewer at ½-inch intervals. Slowly pour orange-lemon mixture over hot cake. Let cool in pan before removing. Wrap airtight and let stand at room temperature 2 days before serving. Serves 18.

SUNSHINE CAKE

With no shortening, this is a basic angel-food or chiffon-type cake that can be filled or layered, if desired.

14 medium eggs, separated
    (1½ cups whites and 1⅛ cups
    yolks)
1 teaspoon cream of tartar
1¼ cups sugar

1 cup cake flour
1 teaspoon vanilla
1 teaspoon grated lemon peel
Confectioners' sugar

Beat egg whites and cream of tartar in large mixing bowl until stiff but not dry. Gradually add ¾ cup sugar. Mix remaining ½ cup sugar with flour and fold lightly into whites a little at a time. In small bowl of mixer beat yolks until very thick and lemon-colored. Add vanilla and lemon peel and fold gently into egg-white mixture until just blended. Pour into ungreased 10 x 4-inch tube pan. Bake in preheated 325°F. oven 1 hour 5 minutes or until top springs back to touch. Invert pan on funnel or narrow-neck bottle and cool cake completely. Turn out and dust with confectioners' sugar. Serves 16.

BLOND FRUITCAKE

This cake freezes well and can be prepared in advance of the holidays.

Grated rind of 1 lemon
1 cup chopped mixed candied fruit
½ cup each, currants, golden raisins and chopped pecans or walnuts
2¼ cups sifted cake flour
1½ teaspoons baking powder
1 package (8 ounces) cream cheese, slightly softened
1 cup butter, slightly softened
1½ cups granulated sugar
4 large eggs
Confectioners' sugar

Butter a 10-inch bundt or tube pan and set aside. Combine rind, fruits and nuts and set aside. Sift flour with baking powder and set aside. Beat cream cheese and butter until fluffy. Gradually beat in granulated sugar. Add eggs, one at a time, beating well after each. Gradually add flour and baking-powder mixture and stir until well blended. Fold fruit-nut mixture into batter and pour into pan. Bake in preheated 325°F. oven 1 hour and 20 minutes, or until done. Let stand in pan on rack 5 minutes, then turn out on rack to cool. Store, well wrapped in plastic wrap and aluminum foil, in cool place. Before serving, dust with confectioners' sugar.

ORANGE-RUM CAKE

2½ cups flour
2 teaspoons baking powder
1 teaspoon baking soda
½ teaspoon salt
1 cup butter or margarine, softened
2 cups sugar
Grated peel of 2 large oranges and 1 lemon
2 eggs
1 cup buttermilk
1 cup finely chopped walnuts
Juice of 2 large oranges (½ cup), strained
Juice of 1 lemon, strained
2 tablespoons light rum

Stir together flour, baking powder, baking soda and salt; set aside. In large bowl of electric mixer cream butter, 1 cup sugar and peels until fluffy. Add eggs, one at a time, and beat after each until thoroughly blended. At low speed add flour mixture alternately with buttermilk. Fold in walnuts. Spread batter evenly in greased 9-inch tube pan. Bake in center of preheated 350°F. oven about 55 to 60 minutes or until pick inserted in center comes out clean, cake shrinks slightly from sides of pan and surface springs back when pressed lightly with finger. Cool pan on rack slightly. In saucepan mix juices, remaining 1 cup sugar and the rum; bring to boil, then pour carefully over cake in pan. Cool, cover; let stand in pan a day or two before serving.

6
CUPCAKES

Easy to serve and delicious to eat, cupcakes are wonderful desserts for children. But their appeal is unlimited—cupcakes are especially welcome at picnics or informal backyard buffets, too. There are many ways to decorate cupcakes for special holidays—with pink frosting and candy hearts on Valentine's Day; with little flags on the Fourth of July; with orange-tinted frosting and candy corn at Halloween—whatever sparks the imagination.
Some recipes, such as the one for Lane Cupcakes, for example, may yield more than what is needed, but keep in mind that plain cupcakes freeze well. Still, you can always halve recipes if desired.

BANANA-NUT CUPCAKES

Extra moist because of the buttermilk and bananas.

2 cups flour
1⅔ cups granulated sugar
1¼ teaspoons baking powder
1¼ teaspoons baking soda
1 teaspoon salt
⅔ cup shortening

⅔ cup buttermilk
3 eggs
1¼ cups mashed bananas
½ cup chopped pecans or
    walnuts
Confectioners' sugar

Blend all ingredients except confectioners' sugar in large bowl of mixer at low speed, scraping bowl constantly. Beat 3 minutes at high speed, scraping bowl occasionally. Line muffin cups with paper or foil liners and fill ⅔ full. Bake in preheated 350°F. oven 25 minutes or until pick inserted in center comes out clean. When cool, dust with confectioners' sugar. Makes 2 dozen.

LANE CUPCAKES

These are great for a crowd, buffet-style, or for bake sales.

1 cup butter, softened
2 cups sugar
1 teaspoon vanilla
3 cups regular all-purpose flour, lightly spooned into cup
3½ teaspoons baking powder
¾ teaspoon salt
1 cup milk

8 egg whites, stiffly beaten
Lane Frosting (page 145; see Note)
Shredded fresh coconut (page 9)
Candied-cherry halves
Angelica or green candied-pineapple strips

Arrange paper-lined foil muffin cups on jellyroll pans. Cream butter. Gradually add sugar, and beat until light and fluffy. Add vanilla. Mix next 3 ingredients and add to butter mixture alternately with milk, beginning and ending with dry ingredients and blending after each addition until smooth. Fold in egg whites. Barely half-fill muffin cups and bake in moderate oven (375°F.) 15 to 20 minutes. Cool on wire rack. To frost, make an indentation in center of each cupcake with teaspoon, removing some of cake (centers can be used for trifle or other dessert). With small spatula, spread at least 2 tablespoons frosting on each cake. Decorate with coconut, half a cherry and angelica. Store, well covered with plastic wrap, then foil, in single layers on jellyroll pans, in cool place. Good keepers. Makes 45. **NOTE:** Substitute another frosting, without liquor, for children's servings.

COCONUT CUPCAKES

A food processor makes easy work of preparing coconut for these delicate and delicious cupcakes.

3 cups shredded coconut (page 9)
3 egg whites
⅔ cup sugar
⅓ cup cake flour

½ teaspoon baking powder
⅛ teaspoon salt
¼ cup finely chopped pecans
Candied cherries, halved

Prepare and set coconut aside. Beat egg whites until foamy; gradually add sugar and continue to beat until stiff peaks form. Fold in coconut, sifted dry ingredients and nuts. Using about 1 tablespoon batter for each, spoon into 2-inch paper-lined foil baking cups and top each with a cherry half; bake in preheated 325°F. oven 25 minutes or until lightly browned. Store in airtight container. Makes 2 dozen.

INDIVIDUAL FRUITCAKES

*This is an excellent dessert for a holiday buffet, and a
gift-giver's delight.*

1 cup flour
1 teaspoon allspice
½ teaspoon cinnamon
¼ teaspoon salt
½ cup butter or margarine
¼ cup packed brown sugar
2 eggs
¼ cup seedless black-raspberry
   preserves

1 cup currants soaked overnight
   in ⅓ cup brandy
1 cup mixed candied fruits
1 cup pecan halves, chopped
   coarse (see Note)
1 tablespoon grated lemon or
   orange peel
15 candied cherries or pecans,
   halved (optional)
⅓ cup brandy

Combine flour, allspice, cinnamon and salt; set aside. In large bowl cream butter and sugar until fluffy. Add eggs; beat at high speed 3 minutes. Blend in preserves. Stir in flour mixture. Fold in currants, fruits, pecans and grated peel. Spoon into 2-inch midget-size foil baking cups set in muffin pans. Top each with candied-cherry half. Bake in preheated 325°F. oven 20 minutes. Cool completely. Spoon about ½ teaspoon brandy over each. Store in airtight container. Makes 30. **NOTE:** Walnuts may be substituted.

KOSSUTH CAKES

*These are basic yellow cupcakes, filled with cream
and frosted.*

½ cup butter, softened
1 cup sugar
2 eggs, beaten
1¾ cups sifted cake flour
2 teaspoons baking powder
½ teaspoon salt

½ cup milk
½ teaspoon vanilla
1 cup heavy cream, whipped and
   sweetened
Chocolate Frosting III
   (page 143)

Cream butter and sugar. Add eggs and beat until light and fluffy. Add sifted dry ingredients alternately with milk, beating after each addition until smooth. Add vanilla. Put in paper-lined 2¾-inch muffin-pan sections and bake in preheated 375°F. oven about 20 minutes. Turn out of pans, cool and peel off papers. Then split almost in two, fill with whipped cream and spread tops with frosting. Makes 12.

CHOCOLATE-OATMEAL CUPCAKES

With buttermilk and oatmeal, these are healthy and delicious.

1½ cups flour
1 teaspoon baking powder
½ teaspoon each, baking soda and salt
¼ cup butter or margarine, softened
1 cup granulated sugar
2 eggs
1 teaspoon vanilla

3 squares (3 ounces) unsweetened chocolate, melted and cooled
⅔ cup buttermilk
½ cup quick-cooking rolled oats
Chocolate Frosting II (optional, page 143)
Nut halves (optional)
Confectioners' sugar (optional)

Stir together flour, baking powder, baking soda and salt; set aside. Cream butter, granulated sugar, eggs and vanilla until fluffy. Stir in chocolate until well blended. Stir in flour mixture alternately with buttermilk until well blended. Stir in oats. Place 2½-inch paper baking cups on cookie sheet and fill cups with batter. Bake in preheated 375°F. oven 12 minutes or until pick inserted in center comes out clean. Cool, frost each with 1 tablespoon frosting and top with nut half, or skip frosting and nut halves and sprinkle cupcakes with confectioners' sugar. Makes 16.

7
TORTES

When describing tortes, it seems that the only thing cake makers agree on is that this is a category with many exceptions and contradictions—as many as there are tortes to be made. One expert will define a torte as a cake using separated eggs and no flour, while another will present a spectacular torte using as much flour as any other type of layer cake. In fact, many tortes do not use flour, but nuts or bread crumbs instead.

From the superb offerings in *Woman's Day*, it is clear to see why, even with the controversy, tortes are among the most popular cakes baked today. Quite different from layer cakes, which in comparison might be described as more of an American dessert tradition, tortes are unusually elegant, readily evocative of the finest cakes baked in Europe.

HUGUENOT TORTE

This is a delicate and moist one-layer cake.

2 eggs	¼ teaspoon salt
1 cup sugar	1 teaspoon vanilla
¼ cup flour	2 cups chopped peeled apples
1 teaspoon baking powder	1 cup finely chopped pecans
½ teaspoon nutmeg	Whipped cream (optional)

In large bowl beat with spoon, until well mixed, eggs, sugar, flour, baking powder, nutmeg, salt and vanilla. Stir in apples and pecans. Bake in greased 9-inch pie plate in preheated 325°F. oven 50 to 60 minutes or until top is cracked and brown and pick inserted in center comes out clean. Spoon into dessert dishes; garnish with whipped cream. Serves 6.

CHOCOLATE-PECAN TORTE

A moist, rich, not very sweet cake, brownielike in texture (not a high, fluffy cake).

1½ cups (9 ounces) semisweet chocolate pieces
½ cup butter, softened
½ cup sugar
4 egg yolks
4 egg whites, stiffly beaten

1 cup pecans, chopped in blender or minced
¼ cup all-purpose flour
½ cup apricot preserves
Whipped cream (optional)

Melt 1 cup chocolate in top of double boiler over hot water. Cool. Cream butter and sugar until light. Add egg yolks, one at a time, beating thoroughly after each. Blend in chocolate. Fold egg whites into batter with nuts and flour. Blend well. Pour into 9-inch layer pan lined on bottom with waxed paper. Bake in moderate oven (350°F.) about 25 minutes. Turn out on cake rack. Spread top and sides with apricot preserves while cake is still warm. Melt remaining chocolate and spread thin layer on top of preserves. Cool cake, cut in thin wedges and serve, with whipped cream if desired.

WALNUT TORTE

2 cups walnut halves
6 eggs, separated
⅛ teaspoon salt

1 cup sugar
1 teaspoon vanilla
Coffee-flavored Whipped Cream (page 149)

Grease bottoms of two 9-inch layer cake pans. Line with waxed paper cut to fit; grease paper and set aside. Toast walnuts in preheated 350°F. oven about 15 minutes; cool. Reserve about 15 walnut halves for decoration. Finely grate remainder in blender or put through nut grinder; set aside. In large bowl of electric mixer beat egg whites and salt at medium speed until soft peaks form. Increase speed to high and gradually beat in sugar, beating until stiff peaks form. Stir vanilla into egg yolks to break up and blend. Fold about a quarter of egg-white mixture into egg yolks, then pour this mixture over remaining egg-white mixture. Sprinkle with walnuts, a few tablespoons at a time, folding in just until no lumps of egg white show through. Divide batter evenly between pans and bake on rack in center of 350°F. oven 30 to 40 minutes or until tops are light brown and pick inserted in center comes out clean. Cool completely in pans, on cake racks. Run small spatula around edges, invert on cake racks and peel off waxed paper. To assemble torte, sandwich layers with about a third of the Coffee-flavored Whipped Cream. Then frost with another third of cream. Put remaining cream in pastry bag with fluted tip and decorate torte as desired. Garnish with reserved walnut halves. Chill at least 1 hour before serving. Serves 10 to 12.

SACHER TORTE

(color plate 7)
*A rich, dark Sacher Torte—a chocolate cake topped
with apricot preserves and covered with a chocolate
glaze.*

½ cup butter or margarine,
    softened
¾ cup sugar
6½ squares (6½ ounces)
    semisweet chocolate, melted
    and cooled
8 eggs, separated, at room
    temperature

1 cup flour, stirred and lightly
    spooned into measuring cup
2 egg whites, at room
    temperature
2 tablespoons apricot jam or
    preserves, slightly heated
Chocolate Icing (page 144)
Whipped-cream rosettes
    (optional)

Grease well 9-inch springform pan; set aside. In large bowl cream butter; gradually beat
in sugar until light and fluffy. Beat in chocolate, then egg yolks, about 2 at a time, until
well blended. Stir in flour. Beat 10 egg whites until stiff but not dry. Blend a third of beaten
whites into chocolate mixture. Gently but thoroughly fold in remaining whites. Pour into
pan; bake on rack in center of preheated 275°F. oven about 1 hour 15 minutes or until
torte pulls away from sides of pan and pick inserted in center comes out clean. Cool in
pan on rack 10 minutes. Run sharp knife around edge; remove rim; cool thoroughly. Cover
loosely with waxed paper; let stand 24 hours; assemble 2 to 3 hours before serving. Put
cake on rack over waxed paper. (Top may be slightly soggy, so cut off thin layer if desired.)
Spread top with jam. Pour Chocolate Icing on center of cake; with large spatula quickly
spread over top and sides. Let set. Decorate top with whipped cream. Serves 12.

LEMON TORTE

Make layers and filling a day ahead.

1 recipe Lemon Cream II (page
    148)
Lemon Genoise Layers

Meringue Frosting (page 142)
2 tablespoons finely chopped
    pistachios or other nuts

LEMON GENOISE LAYERS Follow directions for Genoise Layers (see Opera Torte, page
51), adding 1 teaspoon grated lemon peel and 2 tablespoons lemon juice to butter before
folding into batter. Spread Lemon Cream on layers and stack. Put torte on oven-proof
platter and frost with Meringue Frosting, making decorative swirls with small spatula.
Sprinkle with nuts. Bake in preheated 425°F. oven 5 minutes or until meringue is light
brown.

BRANDY-ORANGE TORTE

A light torte with orange flavor.

6 eggs, separated
⅛ teaspoon salt
1 cup sugar
1 teaspoon grated orange peel
1 tablespoon orange juice
1 cup cake flour, stirred and
  lightly spooned into
  measuring cup

Orange marmalade
½ cup chopped nuts
2 tablespoons brandy
Brandy Whipped Cream I
  (page 149)

Grease bottoms of three 8-inch layer-cake pans and set aside. In large bowl of electric mixer beat egg whites and salt at medium speed until soft peaks form. Increase speed to high and gradually beat in sugar until stiff peaks form. Stir orange peel and juice into egg yolks to break up and blend. Fold about a quarter of egg-white mixture into egg yolks, then pour this mixture over remaining egg-white mixture. Sprinkle with flour, a few tablespoons at a time, folding in after each addition. Divide batter evenly among pans and tap pans twice sharply on table to remove air pockets. Bake on rack in center of preheated 350°F. oven 25 to 30 minutes or until tops are golden brown and spring back when touched lightly with finger. Run small spatula around edges and invert on cake racks. Stir together ½ cup marmalade, the nuts and brandy. To assemble torte, sandwich layers, while still slightly warm, with marmalade-nut filling. Frost with Brandy Whipped Cream I and, if desired, decorate with dabs of additional marmalade. Serves 8 to 10.

SHERRY TORTE

(color plate 2, top)
An elegant dessert that can be assembled in minutes.
Perfect for a special dinner party.

2 cups heavy cream
⅓ cup confectioners' sugar
⅓ cup sherry, divided
Two 8-inch sponge-cake layers,
  purchased or made from mix
  or your own recipe, each split
  in 2 thin layers (see Note)

½ cup chopped toasted almonds
Whipped cream for garnish
  (optional)
Guava jelly for garnish (optional)

In large bowl whip cream until frothy. Gradually add sugar and beat until soft peaks form. Beat in 3 tablespoons sherry until well blended and mixture forms stiff peaks. Drizzle each layer with remaining sherry. Spread cream mixture between layers and over top and sides of torte. Sprinkle almonds on top of torte and press onto sides. Garnish rim with piped or spooned dollops of whipped cream. Top each dollop with dab of jelly. Refrigerate until serving time. Serves 12. **NOTE:** Layers are more easily split when partially frozen. Use a long-bladed serrated knife. To split evenly, insert several picks midway between top and bottom around layer to serve as guides.

OPERA TORTE

A classic torte that's best made a day ahead.

Genoise Layers
1 to 2 tablespoons orange-
   flavored liqueur (optional)
Custard-Cream Filling
   (page 147)

Almond-paste Frosting
   (page 146)
Confectioners' sugar
Whipped cream (optional)

GENOISE LAYERS

6 eggs, separated
1 cup sugar
1 teaspoon vanilla

1 cup cake flour, stirred and
   lightly spooned into
   measuring cup
½ cup butter or margarine,
   melted and cooled

Grease two 9-inch layer-cake pans and set aside. In large bowl of electric mixer beat egg whites at medium speed until soft peaks form. Increase speed to high and gradually beat in sugar, beating well until stiff peaks form. Stir vanilla into egg yolks to break up and blend. Fold about a quarter of egg-white mixture into egg yolks, then pour this mixture over remaining egg-white mixture. Sprinkle with flour, a few tablespoons at a time, folding in gently but thoroughly after each addition. Fold in only the clear part of the butter, discarding milky residue. Divide batter evenly between pans and bake on rack in center of preheated 350°F. oven 25 to 30 minutes or until layers pull away from sides of pans, and tops are golden brown and spring back when touched lightly with finger. Run small spatula around edges; invert on cake racks. While still slightly warm, sprinkle layers with liqueur; cool. Spread tops and sides with filling and stack. Chill until filling is firm, then cover loosely with plastic wrap and chill several hours or overnight. Just before serving, place rolled-out frosting over top and sides of torte, pressing with hands to attach. Sprinkle torte with confectioners' sugar sifted through small tea strainer. Decorate rim and base of torte with whipped cream piped through pastry bag with fluted tip or as desired. Serve well chilled. Serves 16.

ALMOND TORTE

*Rich with almonds and butter cream. Chill several
hours or overnight for best flavor.*

1 cup toasted blanched almonds
½ cup fine dry bread crumbs
6 eggs, separated
⅛ teaspoon salt

1 cup sugar
½ teaspoon almond extract
Praline Butter Cream (page 150)
¼ cup toasted sliced almonds
  (optional)

Grease bottoms of two 9-inch square cake pans. Line with waxed paper cut to fit. Grease paper and set aside. Finely grate almonds in blender or put through nut grinder. Combine with bread crumbs and set aside. In large bowl of electric mixer beat egg whites and salt at medium speed until soft peaks form. Increase speed to high and gradually beat in sugar, beating until stiff peaks form. Stir almond extract into egg yolks to break up and blend. Fold about a quarter of egg-white mixture into egg yolks, then pour this mixture over remaining egg-white mixture. Sprinkle with almond-crumb mixture, a few tablespoons at a time, folding in gently but thoroughly after each addition. Divide batter evenly between pans and bake on rack in center of preheated 350°F. oven 30 to 40 minutes or until tops are light brown and spring back when touched lightly with finger. Cool completely in pans on cake racks. Run small spatula around edges, invert on cake racks and peel off waxed paper. To assemble torte, sandwich layers with about a quarter of the Praline Butter Cream. Frost tops and sides with remaining cream. Chill several hours. Before serving, sprinkle with sliced almonds.

ORANGE TORTE

*A refreshing torte with orange slices. Can be made a
day ahead.*

½ recipe Custard-Cream Filling
  (page 147)
Orange Genoise Layers (see
  Note)
⅓ cup orange juice

4 to 5 oranges, peeled, with all
  white pith removed and thinly
  sliced
Orange Glaze III (page 152)

Spread Custard-Cream Filling on one layer and stack with other layer. Sprinkle top layer with orange juice, then cover with overlapping orange slices, starting at center of torte and working toward edge. Place torte in jellyroll pan. Spoon Orange Glaze over orange slices and sides of torte, scooping up and reapplying glaze that runs down into jellyroll pan. Chill until glaze is firm. Serves 10 to 12. **NOTE:** For **Orange Genoise Layers,** follow directions for Genoise Layers (see Opera Torte, page 51), adding 1 teaspoon orange peel and 2 tablespoons orange juice to melted butter before folding into batter.

8
SPONGE CAKES AND CAKE ROLLS

Sponge cakes and cake rolls are light and appealing, particularly after a large meal. Eggs are the main ingredient in these cakes, which, like angel or chiffon cakes, are also made without shortening. The egg yolks give them a rich golden appearance; the whites, beaten and folded into the batter, account for the delicate, airy texture.

The two sponge cakes, Thistledown and Hungarian Style, offer limitless possibilities for memorable desserts. The cake rolls are as versatile as any dessert could be. Like cream puffs and crêpes, cake rolls provide the "backdrop" for endless filling variations, toppings or frostings. Cake rolls are best handled immediately out of the oven. Carefully invert the sponge layer onto a clean dry towel. Starting at the narrow end of the cake, lift the edge of the towel and coax the cake over onto itself. Roll it up slowly. (When handled warm, the cake will roll up without cracking.) Wrap the towel around the roll and cool thoroughly before filling and decorating.

THISTLEDOWN SPONGE CAKE

A basic sponge cake, to use with any number of fillings and frostings of your choice.

¼ cup all-purpose flour
¼ cup cornstarch
1 teaspoon baking powder
¼ teaspoon salt

4 eggs, separated
¼ cup sugar
Orange Frosting (page 144)

In bowl, mix first 4 ingredients thoroughly. Beat egg whites until stiff. Gradually add sugar and beat until absorbed. Beat in egg yolks. Quickly fold in dry ingredients. Divide into 2 greased 8-inch layer-cake pans and bake in hot oven (400°F.) about 15 minutes. Turn out on racks and cool. Frost.

STRAWBERRY CAKE ROLL

1 cup sifted cake flour
1 teaspoon baking powder
¼ teaspoon salt
3 eggs
1 teaspoon vanilla
1 cup granulated sugar
¼ cup confectioners' sugar

1 cup sliced fresh strawberries
1 pint strawberry ice cream, softened
1 package (1 pound) frozen sliced strawberries, thawed
2 tablespoons brandy (optional)

Sift flour, baking powder and salt. Beat eggs with vanilla until fluffy and light-colored. Gradually beat in granulated sugar. Stir in ¼ cup water. Fold in sifted dry ingredients carefully but thoroughly. Turn into waxed-paper-lined 15 x 10 x 1-inch baking pan. Bake in preheated 350°F. oven 15 minutes or until done. Sift confectioners' sugar evenly onto smooth dish towel. Turn hot cake out on towel and carefully peel off paper. Roll up cake from end, jellyroll fashion; cool. Add fresh strawberries to ice cream. Unroll cake and spread with ice cream mixture; reroll, wrap in foil and freeze. Thaw 10 minutes before serving. When ready to serve, mix thawed berries with brandy and serve as sauce on sliced roll. Serves 8.

CHOCOLATE CREAM ROLL

Make early in the day or a day ahead.

¼ cup cocoa
2 tablespoons flour
6 eggs
1¼ cups confectioners' sugar
1½ teaspoons vanilla
About ¼ cup granulated sugar

Sweetened Whipped Cream (page 148)
Thin Chocolate Glaze (page 151)
Whipped cream (optional)
Chopped pistachio nuts (optional)

Grease 15 x 10 x 1-inch jellyroll pan then line with waxed paper, extending paper at short ends. Grease paper; set pan aside. Stir together cocoa and flour until well blended; set aside. In large bowl of mixer beat eggs at high speed until very light, about 5 minutes. Gradually beat in confectioners' sugar and beat until very fluffy and lemon-colored, about 5 minutes. Fold cocoa mixture and vanilla into egg mixture until well blended. Pour batter into prepared pan and spread evenly. Bake in preheated 350°F. oven 20 minutes or until pick inserted in center comes out clean. Cool in pan on rack 5 minutes. Loosen edges of cake with thin-bladed spatula. Sprinkle clean dish towel generously with granulated sugar and invert cake onto towel. Peel off paper. Starting at short end, roll up cake and towel as for jelly roll. Cool on rack. Unroll. Spread cake with Sweetened Whipped Cream. Reroll *without towel*. Place on platter. Frost with Thin Chocolate Glaze. Chill several hours or overnight. Garnish with dollops of whipped cream and pistachios. Serves 10 to 12.

CHOCOLATE ROLL WITH LEMON FILLING

5 eggs, separated, at room temperature	3 tablespoons unsweetened cocoa
½ cup sugar	Lemon Filling (page 150)
⅓ cup all-purpose flour	Halved pistachio nuts

Line a 15 x 10 x 1-inch jellyroll pan with waxed paper, and grease paper. In large bowl of electric mixer beat egg whites until stiff but not dry. Continue beating while gradually adding ¼ cup sugar. In small bowl of mixer, beat egg yolks with remaining sugar until light and fluffy. Sift flour and cocoa together and thoroughly fold into yolks. Carefully fold this mixture evenly into whites. Spread evenly in lined pan. Bake in hot oven (400°F.) about 10 minutes. Remove from oven and let cool in pan 10 minutes. Turn out onto towel and peel off top paper. Spread with two thirds the Lemon Filling and roll up tightly. (Roll can be wrapped in foil and frozen at this point. Keep remaining third of filling in refrigerator. Remove from refrigerator to soften before frosting thawed roll.) Frost roll. Sprinkle with pistachio nuts.

APRICOT-FILLED WHOLE-WHEAT JELLY ROLL

This is an unusual sponge cake but easy as ever.

6 eggs	1½ teaspoons vanilla
1¼ cups confectioners' sugar plus some for sprinkling on cake	Granulated sugar
	Apricot Filling (page 148)
⅓ cup whole-wheat flour	or ¾ cup apricot preserves

Grease 15 x 10 x 1-inch jellyroll pan; line with waxed paper, extending paper a few inches at narrow ends. Grease paper; set pan aside. In large bowl of mixer beat eggs at high speed until very light, about 5 minutes. Gradually add 1¼ cups confectioners' sugar; beat until very fluffy and lemon-colored, about 5 minutes. Fold in flour and vanilla. Pour into prepared pan; spread evenly. Bake in preheated 350°F. oven 20 to 25 minutes or until pick inserted in center comes out clean. Cool in pan on rack 5 minutes. Loosen edges with knife. Sprinkle a 15-inch length of waxed paper generously with granulated sugar, then invert cake on paper. Carefully peel off waxed paper (baked with cake). If ragged, trim edges of cake. Starting at narrow end, roll up cake and fresh waxed paper as for jelly roll. Cool on rack. Unroll; spread evenly with filling. Reroll *without paper*. Place seam side down on dessert plate. Sift confectioners' sugar on roll. Cut in slices. Serves 8 to 10. **NOTE:** If desired, instead of sprinkling roll with confectioners' sugar, frost with lightly sweetened whipped cream and garnish with toasted slivered almonds. Roll may be made and filled day ahead; wrap airtight. Sugar or frost just before serving.

CHOCOLATE CAKE, HUNGARIAN STYLE

*This light, sponge-type cake contains no flour and has
a mild chocolate flavor.*

5 large eggs, separated
¼ teaspoon salt
Sifted confectioners' sugar
¼ cup sifted unsweetened cocoa
1 teaspoon vanilla

1 cup heavy cream, whipped and
　sweetened
Glossy Chocolate Glaze (page
　151)
Toasted sliced almonds
　(optional)

Separate eggs and beat egg whites with the salt until stiff but not dry. Beat in 1 cup confectioners' sugar, 1 tablespoon at a time, then fold in cocoa. Beat yolks until thick and lemon-colored, and fold into cocoa mixture. Add vanilla. Spread in 15 x 10 x 1-inch pan lined with waxed paper and greased. Bake in moderate oven (350°F.) about 20 minutes. Turn out on towel sprinkled with confectioners' sugar. Very gently peel off waxed paper, using a small spatula to separate cake from paper if it sticks. Cool and cut crosswise in quarters. Put layers together with whipped cream. Spread with glaze; decorate with almonds if desired. Chill and slice.

LEMON ROLL WITH RAISIN-CREAM FILLING

5 eggs, separated at room
　temperature
½ cup granulated sugar
½ cup all-purpose flour
1 teaspoon grated lemon rind
Confectioners' sugar

Raisin-Cream Filling
　(page 148)
Whipped dessert topping
Green candied pineapple
Maraschino cherries

Line a 15 x 10 x 1-inch jellyroll pan with waxed paper, and grease paper. In large bowl of mixer beat egg whites until stiff but not dry. Continue beating while gradually adding ¼ cup sugar. In small bowl of mixer beat egg yolks with remaining sugar until light and fluffy. Gently fold half the whites into yolk mixture with the flour and lemon rind. Carefully fold this mixture evenly into remaining whites. Spread mixture evenly in lined pan. Bake in hot oven (400°F.) about 10 minutes. Remove from oven and let cool in pan 10 minutes. Turn out onto another piece of waxed paper lightly sprinkled with confectioners' sugar. Peel off top paper. Spread baked roll with filling and roll up tightly. (Roll can be wrapped in foil and frozen at this point. Thaw before frosting and decorating.) Frost with dessert topping and decorate with candied pineapple leaves and cherry berries. For berries, cut cherries in half, rinse with water and drain thoroughly on paper towel to avoid staining topping.

BUCHE DE NOEL

*A superb version of the "Yule Log," the traditional
holiday dessert in France, but excellent all year round.*

3 eggs
⅔ cup sugar
4 tablespoons cornstarch
2 tablespoons cocoa
1 teaspoon baking powder
¼ teaspoon salt
Confectioners' sugar

¼ cup finely chopped nuts
¼ cup finely chopped candied
  orange peel
1 cup heavy cream, whipped
Chocolate Frosting II
  (page 143)
Chopped pistachios

Line 15 x 10 x 1-inch jellyroll pan with well-greased waxed paper, leaving 2-inch overhang at each end of pan. In large bowl of electric mixer beat eggs until foamy; gradually add sugar and continue beating about 10 minutes, or until very thick and lemon-colored. Sift together cornstarch, cocoa, baking powder and salt; sift again into egg mixture and fold, blending well. Spread batter in prepared pan and bake in preheated 400°F. oven 8 to 10 minutes or until pick inserted in center comes out clean (do not overbake). Loosen edges with spatula, lift cake from pan by paper ends and invert on kitchen towel sprinkled with confectioners' sugar. Remove paper. Cool 5 minutes, then roll from narrow end, with towel in between. Cool on rack. Fold nuts and the peel into cream. Unroll cake and spread with cream mixture; reroll without towel. Place on serving dish and frost, making decorative grooves with small spatula. Decorate as desired with pistachios. Chill at least 30 minutes. Cut in 1-inch slices. Serves about 8 to 10.

ORANGE ROLL WITH CHOCOLATE-ORANGE FILLING

A wonderful taste combination.

1 recipe Lemon Roll (page 56;
  substitute orange rind for the
  lemon rind)
Confectioners' sugar

Chocolate-Orange Filling (page
  147)
Mandarin oranges

Spread baked roll with two thirds the Chocolate-Orange Filling and roll up tightly. (Roll can be wrapped in foil and frozen at this point. Keep remaining third of filling in refrigerator. Remove from refrigerator to soften before frosting thawed roll.) Use remaining third of filling to frost roll and decorate with very-well drained mandarin oranges.

9
PIES

Pies have been divided into six main categories—fruit, vegetable, chocolate, cheese, nut, and rum-and-cream pies. Making the final selection of pie recipes for this book was a challenge because of the sheer volume of delicious offerings on file. Ultimately, it came down to those pies which offered the best use of fresh, seasonal ingredients, Sliced Lemon or Peach Lattice pies, for example; or gave a new twist to an old favorite, such as Apple-Mince Pie or Pumpkin-Rum Chiffon Pie. In short, the aim was to present a selection of pies that best reflected the diverse and constantly appealing range of recipes that appear every year in *Woman's Day*. There would certainly be a pie for every day of the year if there were room!

All of the basic recipes for pie crusts, as well as many hints for pastry making, are given in Chapter 17. You can substitute any one crust for another in this book; the choice is yours.

Fruit and Berry Pies

Bubbling and steaming with the fragrant juices and flavors of fresh fruits, brought to the table with all eyes turned and opened wide in appreciation, fruit pies are as solid a tradition in American cooking as any type of food could be. All over this land, there is no finer way to celebrate the bounty of the seasons—tart, crisp apples and cranberries, strawberries, blueberries and peaches. Even in winter, citrus and dried fruits are readily available for Lemon Cream, Lime Chiffon pies and others.

Fruit pies are best when baked and served in season, but those who bake in quantity know that any fruits that can be frozen can also first be assembled as a pie, frozen, and served later. Plain fruit or berry pies can be frozen baked or unbaked. Those frozen before baking have fresher flavor as well as crisper crusts, while baked pies will keep longer. Either can be frozen in the metal, foil or oven-proof pie pan in which the pie was prepared. Put it into contact with the freezer surface, and when solidly frozen, cover with a second paper or foil pie pan, wrap and label. Do not cut vents in unbaked pie before freezing. To cook a frozen pie, cut vents and bake in hot oven (425°F.) forty-five to fifty minutes.

Defrost baked pie forty-five minutes at room temperature or in slow oven (300°F.) about thirty minutes. Unbaked pies can be stored in the freezer for three to four months, and baked ones for six to eight months.

In this chapter are all the season's favorite fruits and berries, baked up in scores of new and delicious pies—all destined for many a repeat performance.

LEMON CREAM PIE

Unbaked 9-inch pie shell (page 133)
2 cups sugar
1 tablespoon flour
1 tablespoon cornmeal
4 eggs
¼ cup butter, softened
¼ cup light cream
2 tablespoons grated lemon rind
¼ cup lemon juice
Whipped cream

Prepare crust. Combine sugar, flour and cornmeal in large bowl and toss lightly with fork to mix. Add eggs, butter, cream, lemon rind and juice; beat with rotary or electric beater until smooth and thoroughly blended, and pour into pie shell. Bake on lowest rack in preheated 375°F. oven 45 minutes or until golden brown. Cool. Top with whipped cream.

PEACH CREAM PIE

1 unbaked 9-inch pie shell (page 133)
3 tablespoons flour
⅓ cup sugar
⅛ teaspoon salt
¼ teaspoon nutmeg
¾ cup medium cream
3½ cups sliced peeled firm-ripe peaches

Prepare crust. Chill pie shell and prick a little with fork. Bake in hot oven (400°F.) about 6 minutes. Mix next 4 ingredients, add cream and mix well. Put peaches in shell and pour cream mixture over fruit. Bake in hot oven (400°F.) 40 minutes or until set; cool.

APPLE-MINCE PIE

A savory, spirited version of two all-time favorite pies, combined.

Pastry for 2-crust pie (page 133)
2 cups prepared mincemeat
4 tart apples, peeled, cored and sliced (about 6 cups)
½ cup cognac or brandy
½ cup chopped walnuts
2 tablespoons flour

1 teaspoon grated lemon rind
2 tablespoons lemon juice
2 tablespoons butter or margarine
1 egg beaten with 1 tablespoon water

Prepare crust. Combine mincemeat, apples, cognac, walnuts, flour and lemon rind and juice. Spoon into pastry-lined 9-inch pie pan and dot with butter. Make lattice top, flute rim and brush with egg mixture. Bake on lowest rack in preheated 400°F. oven about 45 minutes or until golden brown. **NOTE:** After about 30 minutes, put foil collar around edge of crust to prevent excessive browning. Cool on wire rack.

PEACH LATTICE PIE

This is an excellent recipe for preparing fresh peach filling in quantity, when the tree-ripened fruit is available in late summer. Freeze and use the filling in pies through the winter.

Butter Pastry (page 135)
9 pounds ripe peaches
3 cups sugar
⅔ cup quick-cooking tapioca
2 teaspoons ascorbic acid (see Note)

1 teaspoon salt
¼ cup lemon juice
2 teaspoons almond extract
1 tablespoon butter or margarine

Prepare crust. Scald peaches, peel and slice. Measure 3 quarts into bowl. Mix sugar, tapioca, ascorbic acid and salt and add to peaches with lemon juice and flavoring. Let stand 15 minutes. **To freeze in pie shapes,** line four 8-inch pie pans with heavy foil, freezer paper or several thicknesses of plastic wrap, allowing lining to extend 5 inches beyond rim of pans. Divide filling evenly among pans, using about 3 cups per pie. Fold extended lining loosely over filling and freeze until firm. Seal lining tightly over fillings. Remove wrapped filling from pans and put back in freezer. **To freeze in containers,** divide filling evenly among 4 freezer containers of about 1½ quart capacity, taking care that filling is at least 1 inch below top of container. Cover and freeze. Filled pies or filling can be stored in freezer up to 6 months. **To bake pies** For each filling, prepare pastry. Roll out half very thin (less than ⅛-inch thick). Line 9-inch pie pan and trim to edge. Roll out remaining pastry very thin and cut in ½-inch strips. If using pie-shaped frozen filling, unwrap and set frozen block of fruit in pastry-lined pan. If using container of filling, thaw at room temperature just until filling can be separated and spread in lined pan. Dot filling with butter. Adjust pastry strips in lattice pattern across top of pie and press ends to edge of bottom crust; flute edges. Bake in preheated 425°F. oven 15 minutes. Reduce heat to 350°F. and bake 40 minutes longer. Cool before cutting. **NOTE:** A commercial antioxidant can be used to prevent browning of fruit if preferred.

SLICED LEMON PIE

This is quite a different way to use fresh lemons in a pie.

Pastry for 2-crust 9-inch pie (page 133)	1¼ cups boiling water
Sugar	Grated peel of 1 lemon
½ cup flour	3 small lemons
¼ teaspoon salt	2 tablespoons butter or margarine

Prepare crust. Mix 1¾ cups sugar, the flour and salt. Add water and beat until smooth. Add grated peel. Cut peel and white membrane from lemons and slice paper-thin, discarding seeds (there should be about ⅔ cup slices). Stir into flour mixture. Line 9-inch pie pan with half the pastry. Pour in filling, dot with butter and adjust top crust. Make a few slits in top crust and sprinkle with 1 tablespoon sugar. Bake in preheated 375°F. oven 45 minutes. Serve slightly warm, topped with ice cream. Serves 6 to 8. **NOTE:** Filling is very soft.

LIME CHIFFON PIE

For a "double-citrus" flavor, substitute 1 teaspoon grated lemon for 1 teaspoon lime in filling.

Baked 9-inch pastry shell (page 133 or 137ff)	¼ cup lime juice
1 envelope unflavored gelatin	4 eggs, separated
1 cup sugar, divided	Grated lime rind
¼ teaspoon salt	Whipped cream

Prepare crust. In top part of small double boiler mix gelatin, ½ cup sugar and the salt. Beat in lime juice, ½ cup water and the egg yolks. Put over simmering water and cook, stirring, until mixture thickens and coats a metal spoon. Remove from heat and add 2 teaspoons rind. Chill until thickened but not firm. Beat egg whites until foamy; gradually add remaining sugar, beating until stiff. Fold into gelatin mixture. Pile in shell and chill until firm. Decorate with whipped cream and additional grated lime rind.

HONEY-STRAWBERRY PIE

Baked 9-inch pie shell
 (page 133 or 137ff)
2 tablespoons cornstarch
½ teaspoon salt
5 cups fresh strawberries,
 washed and hulled

1 envelope unflavored gelatin
¾ cup honey
1 teaspoon grated lemon rind
Honey-sweetened whipped
 cream or vanilla ice cream
 (optional)

Prepare crust. In saucepan mix cornstarch, salt and 2 cups berries, mashed. Gradually stir in ½ cup water. Bring to boil and cook, stirring, over low heat 5 minutes or until thickened and clear. Soften gelatin in ¼ cup water and add with honey and grated rind to first mixture. Cook, stirring, 3 minutes. Remove from heat and cool. Slice remaining berries and fold into mixture. Spoon into shell and chill until firm. Serve plain or top with honey-sweetened whipped cream if desired.

PEAR-RAISIN CRUMB PIE

Be sure to use firm, juicy, ripe pears for the finest flavor.

1 unbaked 9-inch pie shell (page
 133 or 137ff)
6 pears (2 pounds), pared, cored,
 sliced in ½-inch-thick wedges
¼ cup sugar

2 tablespoons cornstarch
1 cup raisins
¼ teaspoon each, nutmeg and
 cinnamon
Crumb Pie Topping (page 153)

Prepare crust. In large bowl mix well pears, sugar, cornstarch, raisins and spices. Turn into pie shell; sprinkle with Crumb Topping. Bake on bottom rack in preheated 400°F. oven 50 minutes or until pears are tender and topping is well browned. Cool on rack. Serve warm or at room temperature. Serves 8.

LIME MERINGUE PIE

A superb citrus taste, summer or winter.

Baked 9-inch pie shell (page 133
 or 137ff)
1 cup plus 6 tablespoons sugar,
 divided
⅓ cup cornstarch
Dash of salt

1½ cups cold water
3 eggs, separated
1 tablespoon butter or margarine
2 teaspoons grated lime peel
¼ cup lime juice (2 limes)
¼ teaspoon cream of tartar

Prepare crust. In medium saucepan mix 1 cup sugar with cornstarch and salt. Gradually stir in water. Stir over moderate heat until mixture boils and thickens. Stir about ¼ cup hot mixture into egg yolks; return to pan; cook and stir 1 minute (do not boil). Remove from heat and stir in butter until melted. Stir in lime peel and juice; set aside. In small bowl beat egg whites with cream of tartar until frothy. Add remaining 6 tablespoons sugar, 2 tablespoons at a time, beating well after each, until stiff peaks form. Pour lime mixture into baked pie shell. Top with meringue, spreading to cover filling completely. Bake in preheated 400°F. oven 10 minutes or until meringue is golden. Cool. Serves 8.

DEEP-DISH NECTARINE OR PEACH PIE

Almond Crust
  (page 137)
2 pounds (about 8) ripe
  nectarines or peaches
2 tablespoons lemon juice
Sugar

⅛ teaspoon salt
1½ tablespoons quick-cooking
  tapioca
Milk
Cream (optional)

Prepare crust. Slice fruit and cover with lemon juice. Combine ½ cup sugar, the salt and tapioca and mix with fruit. Put in 1½-quart casserole. Roll pastry about 1½ inches larger than top of casserole. Cut 3 or 4 gashes in pastry to allow steam to escape, and brush with milk. Put over fruit, trim and turn under. Seal and flute edges. Sprinkle with sugar and bake in preheated 425°F. oven 45 minutes or until browned. Serve warm or cool, with cream if desired. Serves 4.

DEEP-DISH BLUEBERRY PIE

Pastry for 1-crust pie
  (page 133 or 137ff)
2 cartons (9 ounces each) frozen
  dry-packed blueberries (3½
  cups), thawed
1 cup sugar
2 tablespoons flour

1½ teaspoons grated lemon peel
1 tablespoon lemon juice
½ teaspoon cinnamon
¼ teaspoon salt
1 tablespoon butter or margarine
Vanilla ice cream

Prepare crust. Combine blueberries, sugar, flour, peel, juice, cinnamon and salt in 1-quart casserole; dot with butter. Roll out pastry and cut to fit top of dish. Cut slits in pastry and decorate edge with tines of fork. Place on blueberry mixture and bake in preheated 425°F. oven about 25 minutes or until lightly browned. Serve warm, topped with ice cream. Serves 6.

DEEP-DISH CHERRY PIE

*An old-fashioned treat, the kind of cherry pie that
makes you long for fresh cherries all year round.*

Pastry for 9-inch 1-crust pie
  (page 133 or 137ff)
1 quart pitted fresh dark sweet
  cherries
½ cup sugar

Grated rind of ½ lemon
Grated rind of ½ orange
Juice of ½ lemon
⅓ cup light corn syrup
Cream or ice cream (optional)

Prepare crust. Mix all ingredients, except pastry and cream. Put in shallow baking dish about 10 x 6 x 2 inches. Cover with rolled pastry and bake in preheated 425°F. oven 25 minutes or until pastry is lightly browned. Serve warm, with cream if desired. Serves 6.

BLUEBERRY-LEMON CHIFFON PIE

9-inch baked pastry shell (page
  133 or 137ff)
1 envelope unflavored gelatin
¼ cup lemon juice
½ teaspoon salt

¾ cup sugar
3 eggs, separated
1 pint blueberries
Whipped cream (optional)

Prepare crust. Soften gelatin in ½ cup cold water and the lemon juice in top of double boiler. Add salt and ½ cup sugar. Put over boiling water and stir until dissolved. Beat egg yolks until well mixed. Then add hot mixture slowly, stirring. Put back in double boiler and cook, stirring, over low heat until mixture thickens slightly. Remove from heat and chill until mixture begins to set. Beat egg whites until stiff. Gradually add remaining sugar and beat well. Fold in gelatin mixture and blueberries and pour into baked shell. Chill 1½ hours or until set. Spoon whipped cream around edge if desired.

PLUM-PECAN PIE

Baked 9-inch pie shell
  (page 133 or 137ff)
1 cup diced pitted ripe plums
Sugar
¼ cup butter or margarine
2 tablespoons flour

3 eggs, separated
½ teaspoon cinnamon
1 tablespoon grated lemon rind
3 tablespoons lemon juice
¼ teaspoon ground cloves
¾ cup chopped pecans

Plate 1

Nectarine-Orange Bavarian Cream, a soothing,
cooling dessert just right for the peak of summer,
page 100.

Plate 7

The foolproof Sacher Torte, a perfect finale for that special winter dinner party, page 49.

Prepare crust. In saucepan mix ¾ cup water, the plums and ½ cup sugar. Bring to boil and simmer 10 minutes, then stir in butter. Blend ¼ cup water and the flour and stir into first mixture. Cook, stirring, until slightly thickened. Remove from heat and stir in egg yolks, one at a time, beating rapidly after each. Add next 4 ingredients, put back over heat and simmer, stirring, 5 minutes. Chill slightly, then pour into pie shell. Sprinkle with nuts. Beat egg whites until foamy. Gradually add 6 tablespoons sugar and beat until stiff. Pile lightly on pie and bake in preheated 400°F. oven 5 minutes or until golden brown. Cool before cutting. **NOTE:** If preferred, meringue can be omitted. Reserve egg whites for other use and spread thoroughly chilled pie with sweetened whipped cream.

STRAWBERRY SNOWBANK PIE

Baked 9-inch pie shell
   (page 133 or 137ff)
1 quart strawberries
1¼ cups sugar

½ teaspoon cream of tartar
Pinch of salt
2 egg whites
½ teaspoon vanilla

Prepare crust. Wash and hull strawberries and arrange in pie shell, putting prettiest berries in center. Mix sugar, ½ cup water and cream of tartar in saucepan. Cover and bring to boil. Uncover and cook to 240°F. on candy thermometer or until syrup spins a long thread. Add salt to egg whites and beat until stiff. Gradually pour syrup on whites, beating until mixture forms stiff peaks. Add vanilla and pile on pie, leaving center uncovered. Cool, but do not refrigerate because meringue may weep.

TWO-CRUST SOUR-CREAM RAISIN PIE

Golden raisins and a double crust give a new look to an old favorite. The sour "cream" is soured half-and-half.

Two-Crust Lemon Pastry (page
   135)
4 eggs
¾ cup sugar
¼ teaspoon salt
1 teaspoon vanilla

1½ cups soured half-and-half (see
   Note)
1 cup golden raisins
2 teaspoons sugar mixed with
   pinch of nutmeg

Prepare crust. In a large bowl beat eggs slightly. Gradually beat in sugar until light and fluffy. Blend in salt, vanilla and half-and-half. Sprinkle raisins in pie shell; top with filling. Place remaining pastry over filling. Trim and flute edges. Cut slits in top to let steam escape. Lightly dust with nutmeg sugar. Bake in preheated 400°F. oven 20 minutes. Crimp foil over browned edges to keep them from burning. Reduce heat to 350°F. and bake about 15 minutes or until crust is golden brown. Serves 8. **NOTE:** Stir 2 tablespoons white or cider vinegar into half-and-half.

ORANGE CREAM PIE

This pie freezes well. It can be served at the height of the citrus season or any time of year, for that matter.

Graham-Cracker Pie Shell (page 138)
¼ cup finely chopped toasted almonds
4 eggs, separated
¼ cup plus 2 tablespoons sugar, divided
¼ teaspoon salt
⅓ cup orange juice

1 envelope unflavored gelatin
¼ cup cold water
2 tablespoons brandy
1 tablespoon grated orange peel (optional)
Sweetened whipped cream (optional)
Slivered almonds, toasted (optional)

Prepare pie shell, adding almonds to crumbs. In small bowl of mixer beat egg yolks with ¼ cup sugar until thick. Beat in salt and orange juice. In small saucepan mix gelatin and water. Stir over low heat until gelatin dissolves. Stir in yolk mixture. Stir over low heat until mixture thickens slightly and just starts to boil (do not boil). Remove from heat. Stir in brandy and orange peel. Chill until mixture resembles unbeaten egg whites, about 1 hour. Beat egg whites and remaining 2 tablespoons sugar until stiff. Fold into gelatin mixture. Pour into crust. Chill until set, about 4 hours. Garnish with dollops of whipped cream and almonds. Serves 10.

ORANGE CHIFFON PIE

1 baked 9-inch pie crust (page 133 or 137ff)
1 envelope unflavored gelatin
½ cup water
3 eggs, separated
1 tablespoon finely shredded orange peel

1 cup orange juice
2 tablespoons lemon juice
⅓ cup sugar
¼ cup flaked coconut, toasted (optional)

Prepare crust. In small saucepan combine gelatin, water and egg yolks. Cook and stir over low heat until gelatin dissolves and mixture thickens slightly. Remove from heat and beat in peel and juices. Refrigerate or chill over ice water, stirring frequently until thickened. Meanwhile beat whites until stiff but not dry. Gradually beat in sugar until stiff shiny peaks form; fold into thickened gelatin and pour into crust. Top with coconut. Chill several hours or overnight.

BANANA MERINGUE CREAM PIE

Baked 9-inch pie shell
  (page 133 or 137ff)
Sugar
6 tablespoons flour
¼ teaspoon salt
2½ cups milk

3 eggs, separated
1 tablespoon butter or margarine
½ teaspoon vanilla
2 or 3 fully ripe bananas
¼ teaspoon cream of tartar

Prepare crust. Mix ½ cup sugar, the flour and salt in top of double boiler. Add milk and cook, stirring, over boiling water until thickened. Cover and cook, stirring occasionally, 10 minutes. Beat egg yolks slightly. Add a small amount of milk mixture slowly to yolks, put back in double boiler and cook, stirring, 2 minutes. Remove from heat and add butter and vanilla; cool. Slice bananas into shell and cover at once with cooked mixture. Add cream of tartar to egg whites and beat until foamy. Gradually add 6 tablespoons sugar, beating until very stiff. Pile lightly on pie and bake in preheated 400°F. oven 5 minutes or until golden. Cool before cutting.

TWO-CRUST BANANA-RUM PIE

Pastry for 2-crust 9-inch pie
  (page 133)
6 to 8 fully ripe bananas, cut in
  half, then halved lengthwise
¾ cup sugar

1 teaspoon nutmeg
2 tablespoons light rum
1 tablespoon butter or margarine
1 tablespoon evaporated milk

Prepare crust. Line pie pan with pastry, then arrange bananas in pan. Mix sugar and nutmeg and pour over bananas. Sprinkle with rum and dot with butter. Top with pastry, slit in a few places and brush with evaporated milk. Bake in very hot oven (450°F.) 15 minutes, then reduce heat to 350°F. and bake 15 minutes. Serve warm or cool.

FRESH-PEACH PIE

Pastry for 2-crust 9-inch pie
  (page 133)
Sugar
5 cups sliced peeled firm-ripe
  peaches

2 tablespoons quick-cooking
  tapioca
⅛ teaspoon cinnamon
Dash of salt
1 tablespoon lemon juice

Prepare crust. Line 9-inch pie pan with pastry. Combine ¾ cup sugar and remaining ingredients. Pour into pie shell. Cover with pastry, seal and flute edges. With scissors, cut a few slits in top for steam to escape. Sprinkle with 1 teaspoon sugar. Bake in hot oven (400°F.) 40 to 50 minutes.

SPICY RAISIN PIE

Baked 9-inch pie shell (page 133
  or 137ff)
¾ cup packed brown sugar
1 tablespoon cornstarch
½ teaspoon salt
1 teaspoon cinnamon
¼ teaspoon each, ground cloves
  and nutmeg

2 eggs, separated
1 cup dairy sour cream
1 cup raisins
1½ teaspoons lemon juice
½ cup chopped walnuts
¼ cup granulated sugar

Prepare crust. In top part of small double boiler mix first 3 ingredients and spices. Stir in egg yolks and next 3 ingredients. Cook, stirring, over simmering water 10 minutes, or until very thick. Add nuts and pour into shell. Beat egg whites until foamy. Gradually add granulated sugar and beat until stiff. Spread on hot filling, covering edges well. Bake in hot oven (400°F.) 5 minutes or until golden brown. Cool.

Vegetable Pies

As popular as fruit pies, many people bake vegetable pies all winter long. Here are four top-choice recipes from *Woman's Day*, representing the best of pumpkin, butternut squash and carrot pies.

BUTTERNUT-SQUASH PIE

1 unbaked 9-inch pie shell (page
  133 or 137ff)
1 medium butternut squash
  (about 2 pounds), halved and
  seeded
¾ cup water

3 eggs
1 cup half-and-half
¾ cup packed brown sugar
1¼ teaspoons cinnamon
½ teaspoon salt
¼ teaspoon nutmeg

Prepare crust. Place squash cut side down in shallow baking pan. Add water and bake in 400°F. oven 30 to 40 minutes or until tender. Cool until easy to handle, then scrape flesh from shell and mash with fork (there should be 2 to 2½ cups); set aside. Beat eggs, half-and-half, sugar, cinnamon, salt and nutmeg until smooth; stir in squash and pour into pie shell. Bake in 375°F. oven 50 to 55 minutes or until knife inserted in center comes out clean. Cool on rack. Serves 8. **NOTE:** To boil squash bring 1 inch water to boil; add cut-up squash and cook 30 minutes. Drain well and proceed as directed.

PUMPKIN PIE WITH SESAME-SEED CRUST

*For variation, substitute ½ cup honey for brown sugar,
and 2 teaspoons orange rind for lemon extract.*

Sesame Seed Pie Shell (page 137)
2 tablespoons roasted sesame
  seeds
1½ cups canned pumpkin
¾ cup packed light-brown sugar
½ teaspoon ginger
1 teaspoon cinnamon
Dash of ground cloves
½ teaspoon salt

1 cup evaporated milk
2 tablespoons butter or
  margarine
2 eggs, one whole, one separated
½ teaspoon lemon extract
Nutmeg
Sweetened whipped cream and
  slivered Brazil nuts (optional)

NOTE: Before making pastry crust add two tablespoons sesame seeds. Prepare pie crust, adding sesame seeds. Roll to fit 9-inch pie pan, put in pan and flute edges. In saucepan, mix next 8 ingredients and heat, stirring, until butter is melted. Remove from heat and add 1 egg and 1 egg yolk, slightly beaten, and the lemon extract. Beat remaining egg white until stiff and fold in. Pour into lined pan and sprinkle with nutmeg. Bake in hot oven (425°F.) 8 minutes. Turn temperature control to 325°F. and bake 30 minutes longer or until set; cool. If desired, top with whipped cream and sprinkle with nuts.

PUMPKIN-RUM CHIFFON PIE

Orange-Gingersnap Crumb Crust
  (page 139)
¾ cup milk
2 envelopes unflavored gelatin
2 eggs, separated
6 tablespoons sugar

1½ cups canned pumpkin
2 tablespoons dark rum
1 teaspoon cinnamon
¼ teaspoon nutmeg
1 cup heavy cream, whipped
Orange-Almond Pie Topping
  (page 155)

Prepare crust and chill. Put milk in heavy saucepan and sprinkle with gelatin. Let stand a few minutes, then heat gently, stirring until gelatin is dissolved. Beat egg yolks and 4 tablespoons sugar until light and fluffy. When milk begins to boil, stir slowly into egg yolks. Add pumpkin, rum and spices and mix well. Chill in refrigerator, stirring frequently, until very thick, or set in bowl of ice and water. Beat egg whites until soft peaks form. Then gradually add remaining sugar and beat until stiff and glossy. Fold into pumpkin mixture, then fold in whipped cream. Turn into crust and sprinkle with topping. Chill several hours or overnight.

MOCK MINCEMEAT PIE

Carrots are the dominant ingredient. Add ½ cup chopped pecans if desired. This freezes well before or after baking.

Pastry for 2-crust 9-inch pie
  (page 133)
1½ cups grated carrots (about 3
  medium)
1½ cups raisins
1 cup water
¾ cup sugar
3 tablespoons cornstarch
1 teaspoon cinnamon
¼ teaspoon each, cloves,
  allspice, nutmeg and salt

¼ cup butter or margarine,
  melted
2 cups chopped tart apples
  (about 2 large)
1 medium orange, chopped
  (about ⅔ cup)
⅓ cup undiluted orange juice
  concentrate
½ cup grape juice (see Note)
2 to 4 tablespoons vinegar

Prepare crust. In 3-quart saucepan mix carrots, raisins and water. Bring to boil over moderate heat; cook 5 minutes, stirring constantly. Cool slightly. In small bowl mix sugar, cornstarch, spices and salt; set aside. Stir butter, apples, orange and concentrate, grape juice and vinegar into carrot mixture. Stir in sugar mixture. Cook over moderate heat 5 minutes or until thickened and clear. Roll out ⅔ of pastry; fit into bottom of 9-inch pie plate. Pour in carrot mixture. Roll out remaining pastry. Place over filling. Seal edges; cut steam vents. Bake in preheated 375°F. oven 35 minutes or until filling is bubbly. **NOTE:** If more tartness is preferred, substitute cranberry or cherry juice for grape juice.

Chocolate Pies

Seven heavenly pies take chocolate, that all-time favorite ingredient, to spectacular new heights.

DARK-CHOCOLATE MOUSSE PIE

A crustless pie, best chilled overnight.

4 tablespoons finely chopped
  pecans, divided
8 eggs, separated
⅛ teaspoon salt
1 to 2 tablespoons brandy
1 cup sugar

4 squares (4 ounces)
  unsweetened chocolate,
  melted and cooled
½ cup heavy cream
Brandy Whipped Cream II
  (optional, page 149)

Grease 9-inch pie plate well and sprinkle with 3 tablespoons pecans; set aside. In large bowl of mixer beat egg whites at high speed until stiff but not dry; set aside. In small bowl of mixer mix egg yolks, salt and brandy. Add sugar gradually and beat at high speed until thick and light-colored. Add chocolate and beat until well blended. Stir a fourth of the whites into chocolate mixture, then pour chocolate mixture over remaining whites and fold in gently but thoroughly. Pour about half the mixture into prepared pie plate to ½ inch from rim; bake in preheated 350°F. oven 18 to 20 minutes or until still slightly moist when pick is inserted in center; cool on rack. Meanwhile whip cream just until soft peaks form; fold into remaining mousse and chill. Spoon onto cooled baked mousse and chill overnight. Just before serving, decorate with dollops of Brandy Whipped Cream and sprinkle with remaining 1 tablespoon pecans. Serves 8 to 10.

CHOCOLATE CREAM PIE

*Delicious with Meringue or whipped-cream topping—
take your pick! Prepare pie at least 4 hours before
serving but do not prepare a day ahead.*

Chocolate-Walnut Pie Shell
(page 137) or any 9-inch baked
pie shell (page 133)
1¼ cups sugar
⅓ cup cornstarch
¼ teaspoon salt
3 cups milk

3 squares (1 ounce each)
unsweetened chocolate
4 egg yolks, slightly beaten
1 tablespoon vanilla
Topping: Meringue (recipe
follows) or whipped cream

Prepare pie shell; set aside. In large heavy saucepan mix sugar, cornstarch and salt. Gradually stir in milk until smooth. Add chocolate. Stir over medium to medium-low heat until mixture thickens and comes to boil. Gradually blend a little chocolate mixture into yolks; add to remaining chocolate mixture. Stir over very low heat 2 to 3 minutes longer or until slightly thicker. Remove from heat; stir in vanilla. Pour into pie shell. **MERINGUE TOPPING** Immediately heap Meringue (see below) on hot filling, spreading Meringue carefully to seal edge of shell. Bake in preheated 425°F. oven 3 to 5 minutes or until Meringue is lightly browned. Cool slightly, then chill at least 2 hours. If desired, garnish with Chocolate-Walnut Pie-Shell crumbs or shredded chocolate. **WHIPPED-CREAM TOPPING** Place plastic wrap right on filling. Chill pie at least 2 hours. About 1 to 2 hours before serving, remove plastic wrap and spread pie attractively with whipped cream. Serves 8 to 10.
MERINGUE In small bowl of mixer beat until foamy 4 egg whites at room temperature, ¼ teaspoon cream of tartar and dash of salt. Beat in ½ cup sugar, 1 tablespoon at a time, until stiff and glossy. Beat in ½ teaspoon vanilla.

MOCHA-WALNUT PIE

Fudge-nut pie with a hint of coffee added.

Unbaked 9-inch pie shell (page 133 or 137ff)
¼ cup butter or margarine
¾ cup packed brown sugar
3 eggs
1 package (12 ounces) semisweet chocolate pieces, melted

1 teaspoon instant coffee dissolved in a few drops hot water
1 tablespoon dark rum
¼ cup all-purpose flour
1 cup coarsely broken walnuts
½ cup walnut halves
Whipped cream

Prepare crust. Cream butter with sugar, then beat in eggs, one at a time. Add chocolate, coffee and rum. Stir in flour and broken walnuts and turn into pie shell. Sprinkle with walnut halves and bake in preheated 375°F. oven about 25 minutes; cool. Top with whipped cream.

RUM-CHOCOLATE-PECAN PIE

Very rich, with a prominent rum flavor

9-inch pie shell, baked and cooled (page 133 or 137ff)
½ cup butter or margarine, softened
2 egg yolks
2 cups confectioners' sugar
¼ teaspoon salt
¼ cup dark rum
1 teaspoon lemon juice

2 squares (2 ounces) unsweetened chocolate, melted and cooled
2 cups pecan halves, coarsely broken
1 cup heavy cream, whipped
Rum Whipped Cream (optional, page 149)

Prepare crust. In large bowl of mixer combine butter, egg yolks, sugar, salt, rum and lemon juice. Blend at low speed, then beat at high speed until smooth and fluffy. With rubber spatula stir chocolate into butter mixture until well blended. Fold in pecans, then the cream. Pile filling into pie shell and chill overnight. Remove from refrigerator 1 hour before serving. With pastry tube, pipe Rum Whipped Cream on pie to make a decorative topping, or garnish with cream around edge. Serves 12.

CHOCOLATE CHIFFON PIE

A restaurant favorite that you can make even better
at home.

Chocolate-Walnut Pie Shell
   (page 137)
1 envelope unflavored gelatin
Sugar
¼ teaspoon salt
1 cup milk
2 ounces unsweetened chocolate

4 eggs, separated
1 teaspoon vanilla
Sweetened whipped cream (page
   148)
Chocolate syrup (optional)

Prepare crust. In top part of small double boiler mix gelatin, 2 tablespoons sugar and the salt. Add milk and chocolate and put over simmering water. Stir until chocolate melts, then beat with rotary beater until blended. Beat egg yolks and 2 tablespoons sugar together. Stir in small amount of hot mixture, then stir back into double boiler. Cook, stirring, until thickened. Cool, stirring occasionally, then add vanilla. Beat egg whites until foamy. Gradually add ½ cup sugar, beating until stiff but not dry. Fold into gelatin mixture and pile lightly in pie shell. Chill until firm. Top with whipped cream, and drizzle with chocolate syrup if desired.

CHOCOLATE-CHEESE PIE

(color plate 8, bottom)
Best made early in day or night before.

Graham-Cracker Pie Shell (page
   138)
1 package (8 ounces) cream
   cheese, softened
½ cup sugar
Dash of salt
1½ teaspoons vanilla

2 eggs
3 squares (1 ounce each)
   semisweet chocolate, melted
   and cooled slightly
Whipped cream
Chocolate Thins (page 155) or
   shredded chocolate (optional)

Prepare shell; chill. In small bowl of mixer beat cream cheese, sugar, salt and vanilla until well blended. At low speed beat in eggs, one at a time, until smooth. Beat in chocolate. Spread evenly in shell. Bake in preheated 350°F. oven 15 minutes. Turn off heat. Let pie stand in oven 10 minutes longer or until knife inserted in center comes out clean. Cool, then chill. To serve, garnish with dollops of whipped cream, topping each with a Chocolate Thin. Serves 8 to 10.

CHOCOLATE-PECAN PIE

A southern favorite made more delicious with chocolate.

Unbaked 9-inch pie shell (page 133 or 137ff)
¾ cup sugar
1 cup dark corn syrup
½ teaspoon salt
2 tablespoons all-purpose flour
3 eggs

2 tablespoons butter or margarine, melted
3 ounces unsweetened chocolate, melted
1½ teaspoons vanilla
1¾ cups pecan halves
Whipped cream (optional)

Prepare crust. Combine and beat together first 5 ingredients. Add next 4 ingredients and mix well. Pour into pastry shell. Turn some of nuts rounded side up. Bake in preheated 300°F. oven 60 minutes or until just set; cool. Top with whipped cream if desired.

Cheese Pies

Here are three cheese pies, each light, delicately flavored and somewhat less rich than most cheesecakes.

RICOTTA PIE

This is a delicious pie, definitely Italian in flavor.

Baked 9-inch pie shell, chilled (page 133 or 137ff)
2 pounds ricotta cheese
1 cup confectioners' sugar
1 teaspoon vanilla
Dash of cinnamon

2 squares semisweet chocolate, finely shredded
¼ cup each finely chopped candied cherries, citron and sliced almonds

Prepare crust. Beat first 4 ingredients in electric mixer until smooth and creamy. Reserve 2 tablespoons chocolate for top, and stir remainder with other ingredients into first mixture. Pile into shell, sprinkle with reserved chocolate and chill until serving time.

SWEDISH-STYLE CHEESE PIE

An easy crustless pie.

1 tablespoon butter or
  margarine, softened
3 eggs, at room temperature
¼ cup sugar
¼ cup all-purpose flour
¼ cup finely chopped blanched
  almonds

1 teaspoon vanilla or 1 teaspoon
  grated lemon rind
1½ cups pot cheese (dry
  uncreamed cottage cheese) or
  sieved small-curd cottage
  cheese
¾ cup milk
Whipped cream

Spread butter in 9-inch pie pan and set aside. Combine eggs and sugar and beat until light and fluffy. Add flour, almonds, vanilla, cheese and milk and mix well. Pour into pie pan and bake in preheated 300°F. oven 1 hour or until set. Serve slightly warm, topped with preserves and whipped cream. Serves 6.

CHEESE PIE WITH RHUBARB GLAZE

*Not-too-sweet, creamy pie filling with orange flavor,
in a rich, tender pie shell.*

9-inch Sweet-Crisp Pie Shell
  (page 134)
3 eggs, at room temperature
⅓ cup sugar
½ teaspoon salt
8 ounces (1 cup) pot cheese (dry
  uncreamed cottage cheese)
2 tablespoons all-purpose flour

1 cup dairy sour cream
1 teaspoon vanilla
2 teaspoons grated orange rind
Rhubarb Glaze (page 152)
Whipped cream
Finely shredded orange rind
  (optional)
Fresh mint (optional)

Prepare shell, bake and cool. Beat eggs until light; gradually add sugar, beating until light and fluffy. Add salt and pot cheese and beat until well blended. Add flour, sour cream, vanilla and orange rind and mix well. Pour into pie shell and bake in preheated 350°F. oven with rack in center 30 to 40 minutes or until set. Cool on cake rack. Pour Rhubarb Glaze on top and chill 30 minutes or until glaze is firm. Garnish with whipped cream, orange rind and mint. Serves 6 to 8.

Nut Pies

There are many pies that include nuts, but these three stand alone.

COCONUT CREAM PIE

Substitute 1½ cups of fresh shredded coconut (see page 9) for canned, if desired.

Baked 9-inch pie shell
(page 133 or 137ff)
2 cups milk
½ cup sugar
¼ cup flour
½ teaspoon salt
3 egg yolks

2 tablespoons butter or
margarine
2 teaspoons vanilla
1 can (3½ ounces) flaked
coconut
1 cup heavy cream, whipped (or
whipped topping)
Toasted coconut

Prepare crust. Scald 1½ cups milk. Put remaining milk in blender with next 3 ingredients and whirl until well mixed. Add hot milk and whirl at low speed to mix. Pour into saucepan and bring to boil, stirring; boil about 2 minutes. Put egg yolks in blender and whirl a few seconds. Add cooked mixture and whirl a few seconds (do not overblend). Put back in saucepan and cook, stirring, 3 to 4 minutes. Stir in butter, vanilla and coconut; cool. Put into baked pastry shell and chill. Top with whipped cream and toasted coconut. **NOTE:** If preferred, whipped cream can be omitted. Prepare a meringue from 3 egg whites and spread on cooled filling in shell. Sprinkle with untoasted coconut and bake as usual. Serve at room temperature.

WALNUT RUM PIE

Unbaked 9-inch pie shell (page
133 or 137ff)
3 eggs
1 cup light corn syrup
1 cup coarsely chopped walnuts

½ cup sugar
¼ cup light rum
¼ teaspoon salt
Whipped cream

Prepare crust. In medium bowl beat eggs slightly with fork; add syrup, walnuts, sugar, rum and salt, mix well and pour into pie shell. Bake on lowest rack in preheated 325°F. oven about 55 minutes. Cool. Top with whipped cream.

PECAN PIE

Graham-Cracker Pie Shell, (page
   138, see Note)
5 eggs
1¼ cups packed light-brown
   sugar
1 cup heavy cream
1 tablespoon butter or margarine

1 cup coarsely chopped pecans
1 teaspoon vanilla
Sweetened whipped cream
   (optional, page 148)
Chopped pecans to taste
   (optional)

Prepare pie shell. In medium saucepan beat eggs slightly with wire whisk. Stir in brown sugar, cream and butter until smooth. Stir constantly with whisk over low heat until mixture thickens and *just begins* to boil (do not boil). Remove from heat. Stir in pecans and vanilla. Cool 10 minutes. Pour into crust. Chill about 3 hours or until firm. Garnish with whipped cream and pecans. Serves 10 to 12. **NOTE:** Pie is extra delicious, has "nuttier" flavor, if crust is baked in preheated 375°F. oven until lightly browned, about 8 minutes. Cool.

Rum-and-Cream Pies

Rum and cream combined make such a distinct, delicious flavor combination that it was impossible not to include these two pies.

RUM-CREAM PIE

Baked Graham-cracker Crust
   (page 139)
6 egg yolks
¾ cup sugar
2 envelopes unflavored gelatin

1 cup cold water
½ cup dark rum
1¾ cups heavy cream
Whipped cream
Chocolate Curls (page 155)

Prepare crust and set aside. In small bowl, beat egg yolks with wire whisk until light; add sugar gradually and beat until well blended. Sprinkle gelatin over cold water in small saucepan; cook and stir constantly over low heat about 3 minutes or until dissolved. Remove from heat and cool slightly. Briskly beat in egg mixture until well blended; stir in rum. Whip cream until fairly stiff and gently fold in egg mixture; chill in refrigerator until mixture just begins to set. (It will mound when dropped from spoon. If you've chilled it too long and mixture is too firm, beat with wire whisk until smooth.) Spoon into crust and chill pie until firm. Garnish with mound of whipped cream in center and Chocolate Curls.

NESSELRODE PIE

An old-fashioned chiffon-type pie, positively delicious.

Almond-Graham Crust
   (page 139)
¼ cup dark rum
⅓ cup mixed candied fruit,
   chopped
⅓ cup golden raisins, chopped
½ cup sugar, divided
1 envelope unflavored gelatin

¼ teaspoon salt
1½ cups milk
3 eggs, separated
½ cup heavy cream
½ square (½ ounce) semisweet
   chocolate, shaved or shredded
Whipped cream and candied fruit
   for garnish (optional)

Prepare crust. Sprinkle rum over fruit and raisins; set aside. In saucepan combine ¼ cup sugar, the gelatin and salt. Gradually stir in milk. Stir over medium heat until gelatin and sugar dissolve. Beat some warm milk mixture into yolks. Return to saucepan; stir over low heat until mixture thickens and coats metal spoon. Chill until mixture mounds slightly when dropped from spoon. In small bowl beat egg whites until foamy. Gradually beat in remaining ¼ cup sugar. Beat until stiff. Fold into gelatin mixture. In same bowl beat cream until soft peaks form. Fold into gelatin mixture with fruit and rum. Turn into Almond-Graham Crust. Sprinkle with shaved chocolate. Chill until set, several hours or overnight. Garnish with whipped cream and candied fruit. Serves 12.

10
TARTS

Tarts are "as easy as pie" to prepare, but for some reason many people feel they present too much of a challenge. If you have never baked a tart, you are missing out on one of the most satisfying, truly elegant and impressive desserts to serve to guests.

Included here are ten exceptional tart recipes from *Woman's Day*—from a stunning glazed Strawberry Tart to the prize-winning Peach-Pear Flan and more—all surprisingly easy to prepare.

GLAZED STRAWBERRY TART

Rich Tart Pastry Shell (page 133)
2 eggs, separated (yolks also separated)
¾ cup milk
2 teaspoons gelatin
1 whole egg
3 tablespoons flour
3 tablespoons sugar
Dash of salt
½ cup heavy cream
1 teaspoon vanilla
3 cups strawberries, washed and hulled
½ cup red-currant jelly
1 teaspoon water

Prepare pie shell (using 1 egg yolk) and cool. Put milk in heavy saucepan and sprinkle with the gelatin. Beat whole egg, remaining egg yolk, the flour, sugar and salt in small bowl of electric mixer until light and fluffy. Stir into first mixture and heat, stirring, until thickened and mixture bubbles once. Remove from heat and cool over ice water. Beat egg whites until stiff; then whip cream. Fold whites, cream and vanilla into cooled mixture. Spread in pie shell. Arrange berries on pie, pointed end up. Melt jelly with the water over low heat and drizzle over berries. Serve at once or chill not longer than 1 to 2 hours.

BLUEBERRY TART

This is as basic a tart as can be, with a prebaked shell, custard filling and fruit topping. Substitute any fresh fruit of your choice, arranged neatly over the custard.

Rich Tart Pastry Shell (page 133)
Custard Filling (page 147)

1½ cups washed and drained blueberries
1 tablespoon confectioners' sugar

Prepare crust. To assemble tart, spread Custard Filling in pastry shell, then arrange the berries neatly and evenly over surface of custard. Sprinkle with the sugar and refrigerate until ready to serve.

STRAWBERRY TART

(color plate 2, right)
One of the easiest and most delicious of all.

9-inch Baked Graham-cracker Crust (page 139) or any baked pie shell
2 packages (3 ounces each) cream cheese, softened

3 cups whole strawberries, hulled
½ cup red-currant jelly

Prepare crust. Carefully spread cream cheese in crust. Arrange berries, pointed end up, in single layer over cheese. Chill. Heat jelly until smooth and of glaze consistency; spoon over berries. Serve at once or refrigerate. Serves 8.

ORANGE-GINGER TARTS

6 baked medium tart shells, cooled (page 133)
1 envelope unflavored gelatin
½ cup thawed frozen orange-juice concentrate
2 tablespoons sugar

Candied ginger
½ cup heavy cream, whipped
Toasted shredded coconut
Whipped cream
Candied orange peel

Prepare crust. Soften gelatin in ¾ cup cold water, then dissolve over low heat. Add orange-juice concentrate and sugar and mix well. Chill until slightly thickened. Fold in ¼ cup diced ginger and whipped cream and pile in tart shells. Sprinkle with toasted coconut and chill until firm. Decorate with whipped cream and small piece each, ginger and orange peel.

GRASSHOPPER TARTS

Two flavorful liqueurs are blended and combined with whipped cream and other ingredients in a delicious chilled filling.

6 to 8 medium tart shells (page 133) or 1 baked 9-inch pie shell
1 envelope unflavored gelatin
½ cup sugar (divided)
⅛ teaspoon salt

3 eggs, separated
¼ cup green crème de menthe
¼ cup white crème de cacao
1 cup heavy cream, whipped
Additional whipped cream and shaved chocolate (optional)

Prepare shells. In top of double boiler mix together gelatin, ¼ cup sugar and the salt. Stir in ½ cup cold water. Put over boiling water, stirring, until gelatin is dissolved. Beat egg yolks slightly. Pour a small amount at a time of hot gelatin mixture into egg yolks and mix well. Put back over boiling water and cook, stirring, until slightly thickened. Remove from heat and stir in liqueurs. Chill, stirring occasionally, until mixture is consistency of unbeaten egg whites. Beat egg whites until foamy. Gradually add remaining sugar and beat until stiff. Fold gently into gelatin mixture, then fold in whipped cream and mix lightly until blended. Put about ¾ cup filling in each tart shell or pour all of filling into baked 9-inch pie shell. Chill until firm. If desired, top with whipped cream and shaved chocolate.

KENTUCKY DERBY TARTS

Bourbon and pecans give these tarts their distinctive regional flavor.

6 unbaked medium tart shells (page 133)
2 eggs
1 cup granulated sugar
¼ cup butter or margarine, melted
2 tablespoons bourbon
½ teaspoon vanilla

½ cup all-purpose flour
½ cup semisweet chocolate pieces, melted
½ cup chopped pecans
Confectioners' sugar
Whipped cream
12 pecan halves

Prepare shells. Beat eggs slightly. Add granulated sugar and beat in well. Add butter, bourbon and vanilla. Gradually add flour, mixing well. Stir in chocolate and nuts and divide among tart shells. Bake in preheated 350°F. oven about 25 minutes. Cool, then dust lightly with confectioners' sugar. Top each tart with whipped cream and 2 pecan halves.

PEACH-PEAR FLAN

(color plate 7, bottom)
A winner of the Woman's Day *Silver Spoon Award,*
submitted by Cherle Murray. Everything is prepared in
advance except for the glazing.

Special Flan Ring Pastry Shell
  (page 136)
⅓ cup sugar
¼ cup cornstarch
Dash of salt
1¾ cups milk
2 eggs, beaten

1½ teaspoons vanilla
1 can (16 ounces) sliced cling
  peaches, well drained
1 can (16 ounces) sliced Bartlett
  pears, well drained
½ cup apple or peach jelly,
  beaten until smooth

Prepare and bake pastry. In a medium saucepan mix well sugar, cornstarch and salt. Gradually stir in milk. Stir over medium heat until boiling; boil 1 minute. Reduce heat to low. Remove about ¼ cup milk mixture; stir in eggs and return to saucepan. Cook and stir 2 minutes. Remove from heat; stir in vanilla. Cover surface with waxed paper or plastic wrap. Let cool ½ to 1 hour. (Refrigerate for longer storage if not ready to use.) Pour into cooled crust. Cover surface and refrigerate at least 2 hours. Arrange fruit over custard; refrigerate. Just before serving, brush or spoon jelly over fruit to glaze. Serve immediately. Serves 8.

CHRISTMAS TARTS

2½ cups all-purpose flour
2 teaspoons baking powder
1 teaspoon salt
1¼ cups heavy cream, whipped

1 cup butter or margarine,
  softened
Prune Filling (page 150)
1 egg, beaten

Put first 3 ingredients in bowl. Fold in whipped cream, then work in butter, stirring with spoon or working with hands until thoroughly blended. Chill until firm enough to roll. Then roll to ⅛-inch thickness and cut in 4-inch squares. To make stars, cut each corner 1½ inches toward center, put a spoonful of filling in center and fold one split only of alternate corners toward center, pinching edges together. For envelopes, fold dough toward center on two opposite sides, overlapping edges slightly and pressing together. To make triangles, fold two opposite corners together and pinch edges together. Put on cookie sheet and brush with egg. Bake in preheated 400°F. oven 10 to 12 minutes or until golden brown. Makes about 2 dozen.

DOUBLE-PLUM TART

*The smaller the plums, the easier it will be to cut and
serve the tart; you won't have to cut through plum
skins.*

Rich Tart Pastry Shell
  (page 133)
Ripe plums (such as standard,
  sugar, Italian or German),
  about 1½ pounds

1 jar (10 ounces) or 1 cup plum
  jelly
Vanilla (or plain) Confectioners'
  Sugar (page 7)

Prepare crust. Halve and pit plums, cut in ⅜-inch wedges and measure about 3 cups.
Arrange overlapping wedges in a pretty pattern on bottom of crust. Put jelly over low heat,
stirring until melted. Stir to cool slightly, then spoon evenly over plums. Chill just until
jelly sets. Lightly sift sugar over top. Serves 6.

COCONUT TARTS

12 unbaked 3½-inch tart shells
  (page 134)
1 large coconut

1½ cups sugar
5 eggs, beaten
1 teaspoon vanilla

Prepare shells. Pierce eyes of coconut and drain out juice. Add enough water to juice to
make 1 cup. Crack open coconut and grate as directed on page 9. Put coconut in saucepan
with sugar and liquid, bring to boil and simmer 30 minutes; cool. Add to eggs with vanilla
and mix well. Spoon into tart shells and bake in hot oven (425°F.) 10 minutes. Reduce
heat to 350°F. and bake 20 minutes or until firm and golden brown; cool.

11
CHEESECAKES

Cheesecakes are basically a blend of soft, mild white cheese, sugar and eggs. There is probably no other category of baked or chilled dessert that makes a better case for homemade versus store-bought: the proof is in the tasting. As those who love them know, *something* incredibly wonderful happens in a cheesecake to unlock the full flavor of the somewhat bland cheeses—cottage, farmer, ricotta or cream cheese—called for.

Cheesecakes of all types—baked and unbaked, with or without crusts, glazed and garnished with fruit, moist and creamy or light and dry—have long been a main feature in *Woman's Day,* and this chapter presents ten of the most varied—and the very best.

Most cheesecakes are baked in a springform pan, which helps to avoid cracking and breaking when moving the cake to a serving plate. Standard sizes range from seven to nine inches in diameter and are easily found wherever cookware is sold. Rich and filling, cheesecake baked in standard-sized pans will easily serve eight to ten people.

Chapter 17 includes all the crusts for cheesecake. Interchanging crusts with filling recipes is a sure way to arrive at any number of delectable new cakes all your own.

CRUSTLESS CHEESECAKE

As easy as can be. If possible, chill overnight when serving cold.

1 pound cream cheese
1 pound farmer cheese
2 cups sugar
4 eggs
½ cup all-purpose flour

Juice of 1 lemon
1 teaspoon vanilla
½ cup sweet butter, softened
1 pint dairy sour cream

Put all ingredients in large bowl of electric mixer and beat at medium speed 20 minutes or until light and creamy. Pour into buttered 9-inch springform pan and bake in slow oven (325°F.) 1 hour. Then turn off oven temperature control and let cake stand in oven 2 hours. Serve at room temperature or chill if preferred. Serves 12.

CHEESECAKE ITALIAN STYLE

Light and delicate, the top cracks when cooling, and the cake shrinks when refrigerated.

Cookie-dough Crust (page 141)
1 can (20 ounces) crushed
  pineapple, well drained
4 egg whites, at room
  temperature
½ cup sugar
1 pound ricotta cheese, drained
  if necessary

1 package (8 ounces) cream
  cheese, softened
¼ cup all-purpose flour
1 teaspoon vanilla
½ teaspoon salt
2 eggs, at room temperature

Prepare crust, bake and cool. Spread pineapple on crust. Beat egg whites until soft peaks form. Gradually beat in sugar until whites are stiff and shiny; set aside. Beat together cheeses, flour, vanilla and salt until smooth. Add eggs, one at a time, beating well after each. Fold in egg whites carefully but thoroughly. Pour into crust and bake in preheated 300°F. oven 1 hour 10 minutes or until cake tester inserted in center comes out clean. Cool on cake rack, then refrigerate. Run spatula around edge of cake to loosen, then remove sides of pan. Serves 10 to 12.

ALMOND CHEESECAKE

Rich and solid with the crunch of almonds.

Graham-Nut Crust (page 140)
2 packages (8 ounces each)
 cream cheese, softened
Sugar
3 eggs, at room temperature
½ cup ground blanched almonds

½ teaspoon almond extract
⅛ teaspoon salt
1 cup dairy sour cream
1 teaspoon vanilla
Almond Praline Topping (page
 154)

Prepare crust and chill. Beat cheese until fluffy. Gradually beat in ⅔ cup sugar. Add eggs, one at a time, beating well after each, then beat until smooth. Stir in almonds, almond extract and salt. Pour into crust and bake in preheated 350°F. oven 45 minutes. Remove from oven and let stand on rack 20 minutes. Combine sour cream, 3 tablespoons sugar and the vanilla and spread on cake. Put back in oven and bake 10 minutes longer. Cool on rack, then refrigerate. Run spatula around edge of cake to loosen, then remove sides of pan. Sprinkle with Almond Praline Topping. Serves 8 to 10.

PEACH CHEESECAKE

When in season, use fresh peaches, sliced and
sweetened to taste.

Spicy Crumb Crust (page 140)
1 can (30 ounces) cling-peach
 slices, drained
12 ounces cream cheese,
 softened
Sugar

3 eggs
¼ teaspoon salt
¼ teaspoon almond extract
½ teaspoon grated lemon rind
1 cup dairy sour cream
1 teaspoon vanilla

Prepare crust and set aside to cool. Force enough peaches through food mill or coarse sieve to make 1 cup. Reserve remainder for decoration. Cream cheese until fluffy, then beat in ½ cup sugar. Add eggs, one at a time, beating well after each. Beat in peach purée, salt, almond flavoring and lemon rind. Pour into shell and bake in moderate oven (350°F.) 30 minutes or until set. Remove from oven and let stand on cake rack 10 minutes. Mix sour cream, 2 tablespoons sugar and the vanilla and spread on cake. Put back in oven 5 minutes. Cool cake, remove sides of pan and put on serving plate. Decorate with reserved peach slices. Serves 8 to 10. Chill any leftover cake.

ORANGE-COCONUT
REFRIGERATOR CHEESECAKE

Light and fluffy, mild in flavor, not especially sweet.

Coconut Crust (page 141)
1 cup orange juice
2 envelopes unflavored gelatin
¾ cup sugar
2 eggs, at room temperature, separated
½ teaspoon salt

2 cups (1 pound) fine-curd creamed cottage cheese, at room temperature
Grated rind of 1 orange
2 tablespoons lemon juice
1 cup heavy cream, stiffly beaten
1 cup flaked coconut, toasted
1 teaspoon grated orange rind

Prepare crust and chill. Put orange juice in saucepan and sprinkle with the gelatin. Let stand 5 minutes, then stir in sugar, egg yolks and salt. Stir over low heat until sugar and gelatin are dissolved and mixture coats a metal spoon. Set aside to cool. In large bowl of electric mixer beat cheese until fairly smooth. Beat in orange rind, lemon juice and cooled thickened gelatin mixture. Beat egg whites until stiff peaks form, and fold into cheese mixture. Fold in whipped cream. Pour into crust and chill overnight or until firm. Combine toasted coconut and orange rind and sprinkle over top. Run spatula around edge of cake to loosen, then remove sides of pan. Serves 10 to 12.

PINEAPPLE-GLAZED CHEESECAKE

Cookie-dough Crust (page 141; see Note)
5 packages (8 ounces each) cream cheese, softened
1¾ cups sugar
3 tablespoons all-purpose flour
¾ teaspoon grated lemon rind

¼ teaspoon salt
¼ teaspoon vanilla
5 eggs
2 egg yolks
¼ cup heavy cream
Pineapple Glaze (page 152)
Whipped cream and pineapple chunks or tidbits (optional)

Prepare crust. Beat cheese until fluffy. Mix next 5 ingredients and gradually add to cheese, beating constantly. Add eggs and yolks, one at a time, beating thoroughly after each. Gently stir in cream and turn into crust-lined pan. Bake in extremely hot oven (500°F.) 5 to 8 minutes or until top edge of crust is golden. Turn oven control to 200°F. and bake 1 hour longer or until firm. Remove from oven and let stand in pan 3 hours. Remove sides of pan and set cake on serving plate. Spread top with glaze and chill about 2 hours. If desired, decorate with mounds of whipped cream and pineapple chunks. Serves 12 to 16. **NOTE:** Add 1 teaspoon grated lemon rind to dry ingredients for dough.

CINNAMON CHEESECAKE

Creamy texture with a rich crust; shrinks as it cools.

Cookie-dough Crust (page 141)
2 packages (8 ounces each)
   cream cheese, softened
¾ cup sugar
2 tablespoons each, grated
   orange and lemon rinds

1 tablespoon lemon juice
1 teaspoon vanilla
4 eggs, at room temperature
Cinnamon Sugar

Prepare crust, bake and cool. Beat together cheese, sugar, grated rinds, lemon juice and vanilla until smooth. Add eggs, one at a time, beating well after each. Pour into crust and sprinkle with Cinnamon Sugar. Bake in preheated 350°F. oven 45 minutes or until set. Cool on cake rack, then chill, if preferred. Run spatula around edge of cake to loosen, then remove sides of pan. Serves 8 to 10.

CINNAMON SUGAR Mix together 3 tablespoons sugar and 1 teaspoon cinnamon.

CHOCOLATE CHEESECAKE

A cake with a smooth, solid texture; it falls and cracks as it cools.

Chocolate-wafer Crust (page 141)
3 packages (8 ounces each)
   cream cheese, softened
¾ cup sugar
3 eggs
1 package (8 ounces) semisweet
   chocolate squares, melted

½ cup strong black coffee,
   cooled
½ cup dairy sour cream
1 teaspoon vanilla
⅛ teaspoon salt
Unsweetened whipped cream
   (optional)
Chocolate Curls (optional, page
   155)

Prepare crust and chill. Beat cheese in large bowl of electric mixer until light and fluffy. Gradually beat in sugar. Add eggs, one at a time, beating well after each. Beat in chocolate, coffee, sour cream, vanilla and salt until smooth. Pour into prepared pan and bake in preheated 350°F. oven 1 hour or until firm in center. Cool on cake rack, then chill if preferred. Run spatula around edge of cake to loosen, then remove sides of pan. Garnish with whipped cream and Chocolate Curls if desired. Serves 16.

MARBLE CHEESECAKE

*A chocolate-cinnamon crust, creamy filling and
chocolate marble.*

**Chocolate-Cinnamon Crust
  (page 141)**
**12 ounces cream cheese,
  softened**
½ cup sugar
1 teaspoon grated lemon rind

2 eggs
1½ cups dairy sour cream
**1 package (8 ounces) semisweet
  chocolate squares or 1⅓ cups
  pieces, melted**

Prepare crust. Combine first 3 ingredients and beat until well blended. Beat in eggs, then stir in sour cream until smooth. Add chocolate and stir with fork until mixture is marbleized. Pour into crust and bake in preheated 350°F. oven 35 to 40 minutes or until set. Chill 2 hours or longer, then remove rim. Serves 10.

COFFEE CHEESECAKE

*This cake has a creamy, light texture and a rich coffee
flavor. The top cracks during baking, and the cake
shrinks when cool.*

Vanilla-wafer Crust (page 140)
**3 packages (8 ounces each)
  cream cheese, softened**
¾ cup sugar
3 eggs, at room temperature

**1 tablespoon plus 1 teaspoon
  instant coffee granules**
2 tablespoons hot water
½ cup dairy sour cream

Prepare crust and chill. Beat cheese until light and fluffy. Gradually beat in sugar. Add eggs, one at a time, beating well after each. Dissolve coffee in the hot water and beat into mixture with sour cream. Pour into crust and bake in preheated 350°F. oven 1 hour or until firm in center. Cool on cake rack, then chill. Run spatula around edge of cake to loosen, then remove sides of pan. Serves 10 to 12.

12
CREAM PUFFS AND
ÉCLAIRS

While cream puffs and éclairs are delicious with the standard whipped cream or custard fillings, they are often overlooked as the basis for many more pleasing, distinctive desserts. Filled with marinated fresh fruits, homemade sherbets or ices or frozen fruit yogurt, their calorie-rich reputation is transformed into something light and refreshing.

Because cream-puff pastry can be made several hours ahead of time, cream puffs are well-suited for dinner parties. And with the following foolproof pastry recipe, given step-by-step, cream puffs or éclairs could not be an easier dessert to serve. When the shells are made several hours ahead of serving, they will stay crisp if left uncovered. They can also be frozen for future use, packed loosely and sealed airtight in plastic bags. When ready to use, heat the puffs in a 350°F. oven for eight to ten minutes to crisp them. Cool before filling.

Choose fillings and frostings suggested in this chapter or use your own favorites. Turn to chapters 18 and 19 for other ideas.

FOOLPROOF CREAM-PUFF PASTRY

Use an electric mixer if available, or beat by hand with wooden spoon. Use standard measuring cups and spoons for measuring ingredients, leveling off top with edge of spatula. Give recipe your undivided attention.

4 large eggs or ⅞ cup if another
   size is used
1 cup unsifted all-purpose flour
   (not instant or unbleached)
1 cup water
½ cup (1 stick) butter or
   margarine (not soft, whipped
   or salt-free)

1 teaspoon granulated sugar
⅛ teaspoon salt
Vanilla Cream Filling (page 92)
   or other filling
Confectioners' sugar or frosting

Preheat oven to 425°F. (If you are in doubt about the accuracy of your oven, use oven thermometer and regulate heat. Correct temperature is important.) Take eggs directly from refrigerator and break into small bowl. Spoon flour lightly into measuring cup and level off top with side of spatula. Put water, butter, granulated sugar and salt in deep, heavy 2-quart saucepan. Put over medium heat until butter melts, then bring to rolling boil over high heat. Remove from heat and add flour all at once. Beat vigorously with wooden spoon until thoroughly blended. Stir over medium heat 2 minutes or until mixture forms a ball, leaves sides of pan and begins to form a film on bottom of pan. Put mixture in large bowl of electric mixer and beat at low speed about 1 minute to cool slightly. Add eggs all at once and beat at medium speed, scraping sides of bowl while beating until batter is thick and begins to cling to beaters (about 2 minutes). Beat about 2 minutes longer, lifting up beaters slightly several times to allow dough to run off a bit. The final time, let dough work its way off beaters (mixture will be very stiff).

To Make by Hand Remove mixture from heat and stir gently about 2 minutes to cool slightly. Add slightly beaten eggs by fourths and beat well with wooden spoon after each addition until egg is completely absorbed. Then beat 2 minutes or until smooth and velvety. Using 2 tablespoons, drop mixture in 12 mounds, heaping up in center, about 2 inches apart on ungreased cookie sheet (a 17 x 14-inch sheet will hold 12 puffs). Bake in 425°F. oven 20 minutes, then turn oven control to 375°F. and bake 15 minutes longer (do not underbake). Turn off oven. Remove puffs from oven and, with small knife, make a small slit in side of each. Then put back in oven leaving door open slightly, about 10 minutes. Remove to cake rack, loosening with spatula, and cool away from drafts. When cold, split with sharp knife and pull out any soft filament of dough. Not more than 2 hours before serving, fill with preferred filling and sprinkle with confectioners' sugar or frost. Store in refrigerator until ready to serve (do not cover, because puffs will become soft). Put ice-cream-filled puffs in freezer.

ÉCLAIRS Prepare dough as for cream puffs. With spoon and knife, shape in 12 fingers 4½ x 1 inch on ungreased cookie sheet. Or force through pastry bag, using tip with one large hole. (If possible, put all dough in bag at once.) Bake and fill as directed for cream puffs.

Fillings and Frostings for Cream Puffs and Éclairs

Woman's Day offered the following recipes for a quantity of 12 puffs or éclairs; turn also to chapters 18 and 19 for other fillings, frostings, toppings and sauces—all perfectly suited for puffs or éclairs.

VANILLA CREAM FILLING

3 cups milk
¾ cup sugar
6 tablespoons cornstarch
½ teaspoon salt

3 eggs, slightly beaten
1 tablespoon butter or margarine
2 teaspoons vanilla

Scald milk in top part of double boiler over boiling water. Mix sugar, cornstarch and salt and stir into milk. Cook and stir until thickened. Cover and cook, stirring occasionally, 15 minutes longer. Stir small amount of mixture into eggs, then stir egg mixture into mixture in double boiler and cook and stir 5 minutes. Remove from heat and, if not smooth, beat with rotary beater. Add butter and stir until melted. Cool and add vanilla, then chill. Makes enough filling for 12 puffs or éclairs.

CHOCOLATE CREAM FILLING Follow above recipe, melting 3 squares unsweetened chocolate in the milk. Beat smooth with rotary beater and proceed as directed.

COFFEE CREAM FILLING Follow recipe for vanilla filling, adding 2 tablespoons instant coffee (not freeze-dried) to sugar mixture. Reduce vanilla to 1 teaspoon.

FLUFFY CREAM FILLING Follow any recipe above, reducing milk to 2½ cups. Just before using, fold ½ cup heavy cream, whipped, into chilled mixture.

OTHER FILLINGS
• For 12 cream puffs, whip 2 cups heavy cream until quite stiff. Sweeten to taste with sugar and add 1 teaspoon vanilla.
• Omit vanilla in whipped cream and fold in a few sliced strawberries or some diced canned peaches, apricots or pineapple.
• Fill puffs with thawed frozen vanilla, chocolate or butterscotch pudding.

Frosted pastries can be sprinkled with coconut, chopped nuts or chocolate shot.

CHOCOLATE FROSTING Melt together 1½ squares unsweetened chocolate and 1 teaspoon butter. Stir in 1½ cups confectioners' sugar and 2½ to 3 tablespoons hot water. Mix until smooth.

BUTTERSCOTCH FROSTING In top part of double boiler put ¼ cup butter, ½ cup packed light-brown sugar, ⅛ teaspoon salt and ⅓ cup undiluted evaporated milk. Cook over boiling water, stirring, until smooth. Cool slightly, then add 1½ cups confectioners' sugar and ½ teaspoon vanilla; beat with spoon until smooth.

COFFEE FROSTING Cream well ¼ cup butter or margarine. Dissolve 2 teaspoons instant coffee (not freeze-dried) in 1 tablespoon water. Add alternately to butter with about 1½ cups confectioners' sugar, beating well with wooden spoon about 2 minutes. Stir in dash of salt and 1 teaspoon vanilla. Let stand a few minutes, then stir and spread.

CREAM PUFFS WITH BANANA WHIPPED CREAM

(color plate 4, top)
This recipe makes half the amount of cream-puff
pastry given previously.

½ cup water	1 cup heavy cream
¼ cup butter or margarine	2 teaspoons vanilla, or to taste
Dash of salt	3 medium-size very ripe
½ cup flour	bananas, diced (2 cups)
2 eggs	

In heavy medium-size saucepan combine water, butter and salt. Heat over medium heat until butter melts. Increase heat to high and bring mixture to rolling boil. Remove from heat and add flour. Beat vigorously until blended. Stir over medium heat 2 minutes or until mixture forms a ball, leaves sides of pan and begins to form a film on bottom of pan. Turn mixture into small bowl of mixer and beat at low speed about 1 minute to cool slightly. Add eggs and beat at medium speed until dough is very stiff, about 4 minutes, lifting beaters slightly occasionally. (Or after mixture forms ball, remove from heat and cool slightly. Add eggs, one at a time, and beat with wooden spoon until dough is very stiff.) Drop dough by tablespoonfuls in 6 mounds about 2 inches apart on ungreased cookie sheet, heaping up centers. Bake in preheated 425°F. oven 20 minutes. Reduce temperature to 375°F. and bake 15 minutes longer or until feather-light and golden brown. Turn off heat. Remove puffs and make small slit in side of each. Return to oven 10 minutes, leaving door ajar. Cool on rack. In small chilled bowl whip cream and vanilla until stiff; fold in bananas. Split cream puffs; pull out and discard soft portions of dough. Fill with banana whipped cream. Serves 6.

13
CRÊPES

As a dessert, crêpes share the same distinction as cream puffs by serving as a simple and delicious base for any number of sweet fillings and toppings. Included in this chapter are several all-purpose dessert crêpes—two brandied versions, for the ever-popular Crêpes Suzette and Strawberry Crêpes (both flamed); Vanilla Crêpes and Chocolate Dessert Crêpes. Interchange these with the fillings to suit your taste.
In addition to the crêpe recipes, there is also a recipe here for Apple Pancake Pie, an unusually tasty skillet turnover.

CRÊPES SUZETTE

1 cup flour	2 tablespoons brandy
1 teaspoon sugar	Orange Butter
¼ teaspoon salt	1 tablespoon sugar and ¼ cup
¾ cup milk	brandy for flaming
⅔ cup cold water	Strips of orange peel for garnish
3 egg yolks	(optional)
2 tablespoons butter, melted	

In large bowl of mixer combine flour, sugar and salt. Gradually beat in milk and water until smooth. Beat in egg yolks. Cover and chill overnight. Just before baking beat in butter and 2 tablespoons of brandy. Heat well-seasoned 5-, 6- or 7-inch crêpe pan over medium heat until hot. Pour in scant ¼ cup batter, quickly tilting pan to distribute batter evenly. When light brown on bottom and edges are crisp, turn and cook briefly on other side (do not brown). Turn out bottom side up on waxed paper. Bake remaining crêpes; stack between sheets of waxed paper. (Makes about 12.) Spread bottom side of each crêpe with about 1 tablespoon Orange Butter. Fold in half, then in quarters. Spread remaining Orange Butter in bottom of 10-inch chafing pan or skillet. Arrange crêpes over Orange Butter. Just before serving, sprinkle with sugar and heat in preheated 400°F. oven 5 minutes. Put chafing pan over flame of chafing burner or gas range. Pour brandy around edge of pan. Stand back and ignite brandy with lighted long match. Shake pan gently back and forth, spooning sauce over crêpes until flame dies. Garnish with orange peel. Serve at once. Serves 4.

To Make Orange Butter:

¾ cup butter, softened
½ cup sugar
1 tablespoon finely grated orange
  peel

⅓ cup orange juice
2 tablespoons orange liqueur

In small bowl of mixer cream butter and sugar until light and fluffy. Beat in orange peel, then gradually beat in juice and liqueur until well blended.

STRAWBERRY CRÊPES

*To prepare ahead, make crêpes and refrigerate. Wrap
in foil and reheat in slow oven.*

2 eggs, well beaten
½ cup milk
½ cup all-purpose flour
1 tablespoon cognac
½ teaspoon salt
Sugar

Butter or margarine
8 ounces cream cheese, softened
1 cup dairy sour cream
1 quart strawberries, washed,
  hulled and sliced
⅓ cup kirsch

Mix well first 5 ingredients and 1 teaspoon sugar. Let stand in refrigerator 2 to 3 hours. (Batter should be the consistency of heavy cream when baked. If too thick, add a little more milk.) Brush a 7- or 8-inch skillet with butter. Pour 1 generous tablespoonful batter at a time into skillet and bake, turning once. Keep crêpes warm. Mash cheese with fork, then mix with sour cream. Put 1 rounded tablespoonful on each crêpe and roll up. In skillet or chafing dish, heat berries with 1 cup sugar and 2 tablespoons butter, stirring until sugar is dissolved. Arrange 2 crêpes on each serving plate. Pour kirsch over berries and ignite. Serve on crêpes. Serves 6.

VANILLA CRÊPES

Substitute one teaspoon vanilla for cognac in crêpe recipe above.

CHOCOLATE DESSERT CRÊPES

A special crêpe batter for chocolate enthusiasts. Good with ice cream, whipped cream. If you don't have buttermilk, add 1 tablespoon lemon juice to 1¼ cups regular milk.

3 eggs
1 cup flour
2 tablespoons sugar
2 tablespoons cocoa

1¼ cups buttermilk
2 tablespoons butter or margarine, melted

Mixer or whisk method In medium bowl beat eggs. Add flour, sugar and cocoa alternately with buttermilk, beating with mixer or whisk until smooth. Beat in butter.
Blender method Whirl all ingredients in blender about 1 minute. Scrape down sides with rubber spatula. Blend 15 seconds or until smooth.
Both methods Refrigerate batter about 1 hour. Bake in traditional crêpe pan or on upside-down crêpe griddle. Makes 18 to 22 6-inch crêpes.

FRUIT-FILLED CRÊPES WITH PINEAPPLE SAUCE

For Crepes:
2 eggs
½ teaspoon salt
½ cup each, milk and water
¼ cup each, cornstarch and flour
2 tablespoons butter or margarine, melted
For Filling and Sauce:
1 can (6 ounces) frozen pineapple-juice concentrate diluted with 1 can water, divided

Juice of 1 small lemon
½ cup chopped dates
1 large red apple, cored and chopped
1 medium-size ripe pear, cored and chopped
1 medium banana, sliced
1 tablespoon butter or margarine
1 cup heavy cream whipped with 1 teaspoon vanilla (optional)

In bowl combine eggs and salt. Beat in mixture of milk and water alternately with mixture of cornstarch and flour until smooth. Stir in melted butter or margarine. Let stand at least 30 minutes. Stir batter. Using scant ¼ cup measure for each crêpe, bake in lightly greased 7- or 8-inch crêpe pan or use crêpe maker, following manufacturer's directions. In bowl combine ¼ cup pineapple juice, the lemon juice, dates, apple, pear and banana. Toss gently to mix. Spoon about ¼ cup sauce on each crêpe. Roll up; place seam side down in greased shallow broiler-proof baking dish. Spoon any remaining fruit mixture over crêpes; set aside. In small saucepan cook remaining pineapple juice over high heat *without stirring* until reduced to half. Add butter; stir until melted. Spoon over crêpes. Broil about 6 inches from heat source until lightly browned and heated, about 3 minutes. Serve topped with whipped cream. Serves 4 or 5.

APPLE PANCAKE PIE

When this puffed pancake is folded over apples, it forms a top "crust." Serve for a special dessert when the apple season is at its peak.

Butter or margarine
4 tart cooking apples, peeled, quartered, cored and thinly sliced lengthwise
10 tablespoons sugar
¼ teaspoon ground cinnamon
⅛ teaspoon ground nutmeg
2 eggs
½ cup milk
¼ teaspoon salt
½ cup stirred flour

Melt 6 tablespoons butter in large skillet over medium heat and sauté apples 5 minutes. Mix 6 tablespoons sugar with cinnamon and nutmeg, sprinkle over apples, cover and cook over low heat 10 minutes, turning once or twice. Beat eggs, then beat in milk and salt; add flour and beat just until batter is smooth. In separate heavy 10- to 11-inch frying pan, melt 1 tablespoon butter to coat bottom of pan. Pour in batter. Bake in preheated 450°F. oven 15 minutes. (When batter puffs in center, prick with fork; repeat when necessary.) Reduce heat to 350°F. and bake 10 minutes more. Spoon 2 tablespoons melted butter evenly over pancake and sprinkle with 2 tablespoons sugar. Spoon apple mixture over half the pancake, then fold other half over top. Sprinkle with remaining 2 tablespoons sugar. Cut in 6 wedges with kitchen shears and serve immediately. **NOTE:** If desired, sprinkle confectioners' sugar instead of granulated over pancake.

14
CREAMS, CUSTARDS, MOUSSES, PUDDINGS AND PUDDING CAKES

Here are the "heavenly desserts"—shimmering custards and creams, frothy, rich mousses, glistening puddings and pudding cakes—the pride of every cook and hostess.

Whether thickened with eggs, cream and/or gelatin, baked or chilled, many of the recipes, such as Almond Custard or Chocolate Mousse with Mocha Whipped Cream, could not be easier. It is just a matter of blending ingredients and baking or chilling them until set. Others, like Crème Caramel or Chocolate Bavarian Cream, are well worth a bit more time and effort, and a few special skills—heating sugar syrup or cooking eggs as thickeners, for example. With egg custards and desserts, careful, slow cooking is the key, whether the end result is soft-cooked on the stove or firm in the oven.

Apart from the detailed instructions given with each recipe, review the hints and basic procedures given in Chapter 1.

LEMON BAVARIAN WITH RASPBERRY SAUCE

(color plate 2, bottom left)

2 packages (3 ounces each)
   lemon gelatin
2 cups boiling water
4 cups ice cubes
1 cup heavy cream, whipped

2 packages (10 ounces each)
   frozen raspberries or
   strawberries in syrup, thawed,
   or 1 pint fresh raspberries or
   strawberries, sweetened to
   taste

In large bowl stir gelatin and boiling water until gelatin is dissolved. Add ice and stir until gelatin thickens; discard any remaining ice. Gently fold in whipped cream. Turn into 8-

cup mold: chill several hours or overnight or until firm. Mash berries or purée in blender or food mill. Put through strainer to remove seeds if desired. Drizzle some sauce over mold; pass remainder. Serves 12 to 16.

BLENDER LEMON OR LIME BAVARIAN CREAM

(color plate 6, top)

1 package (3 ounces) ladyfingers, split (optional)
2 envelopes unflavored gelatin
¼ cup cold water
Thin strips of peel from 1 medium lemon or lime
½ cup boiling water
¼ cup lemon or lime juice

1 cup sugar
¼ teaspoon salt
3 eggs
1 cup heavy cream, half-and-half or lemon-flavor yogurt
1½ cups ice cubes
Lemon slices and fresh mint sprigs (optional)

Line sides and bottom of 1½-quart glass serving bowl with ladyfingers, rounded sides up; set aside. In blender sprinkle gelatin over cold water. Let stand 1 minute. Add peel, boiling water and juice. Blend at low speed until gelatin dissolves and peel is grated fine. Add sugar, salt, eggs and cream. Blend at high speed, adding ice cubes, one at a time, until ice is melted. Pour at once into prepared serving bowl. Chill 15 minutes or until set. Garnish with lemon slices and fresh mint. Serves 6.

CHOCOLATE BAVARIAN CREAM

A perfect company dessert—garnish with whipped cream. Can be made a day ahead.

¾ cup sugar, divided
¼ cup cocoa
1 envelope unflavored gelatin
1½ cups milk

3 eggs, separated, at room temperature
1 teaspoon vanilla
¾ cup heavy cream

In top of double boiler over simmering water or in heavy saucepan over medium-low heat mix well ½ cup sugar, the cocoa and gelatin; stir in milk. Cook just to boiling. Stir ½ cup cocoa mixture into yolks, then stir into pan mixture. Cook and stir until mixture coats metal spoon, 10 to 15 minutes. Remove from heat; stir in vanilla. Cool, then chill until mixture mounds when dropped from spoon, stirring occasionally. In small bowl of mixer beat egg whites and remaining ¼ cup sugar until stiff peaks form; set aside. In another bowl whip cream until stiff peaks form. Fold egg-white mixture and cream into chilled custard. Spoon into chilled 6-cup mold. Chill until firm, 2 to 4 hours. Unmold on serving dish. Serves 6.

NECTARINE-ORANGE BAVARIAN CREAM

(color plate 1)

2 envelopes unflavored gelatin	4 large nectarines, divided
⅔ cup sugar, divided	2 cups heavy cream, divided
¾ cup orange juice	½ teaspoon vanilla
2 egg yolks	½ cup blueberries (optional)

In heavy saucepan mix gelatin and ⅓ cup sugar. Stir in orange juice and egg yolks; blend well. Let stand 1 minute. Stir over low heat until gelatin is completely dissolved and mixture thickens slightly, 5 to 7 minutes. Remove from heat. Slice 2 nectarines and purée in blender with remaining ⅓ cup sugar. Stir into gelatin mixture. Chill, stirring occasionally, until mixture mounds slightly when dropped from a spoon. Whip 1½ cups cream until stiff. Fold in fruit-gelatin mixture. Pour into 5-cup ring or other mold. Chill until firm. Unmold on platter. Slice remaining 2 nectarines. Whip remaining ½ cup cream until stiff; fold in vanilla. If desired, put in pastry bag and pipe out large rosettes, or spoon dollops on mold and garnish with nectarine slices and blueberries. Serves 6 to 8.

JELLIED STRAWBERRY CREAM

2 envelopes unflavored gelatin	1 teaspoon grated lemon or
½ cup cold water	orange peel
1 cup boiling water	1 to 2 tablespoons lemon or
¼ cup sugar	orange juice
1 pint vanilla ice cream,	1 pint strawberries, divided, with
softened	1 cup chopped coarse
	½ cup heavy cream, whipped

In large mixing bowl sprinkle gelatin over cold water; let stand until softened, a few minutes. Add boiling water and sugar and stir until dissolved. Add ice cream, lemon peel and juice and beat with whisk until ice cream melts. Let stand until mixture mounds *slightly* when dropped from spoon, about 3 to 5 minutes (happens quickly because of cold ice cream). Fold in chopped strawberries and whipped cream. Spoon into glass serving bowl. Chill until set, about 30 minutes. Garnish with remaining whole strawberries. Serves 6.

CRÈME CARAMEL

The velvety French classic prepared as a large wheel.
Make a day ahead.

½ cup plus 3 tablespoons sugar
4 eggs
1 teaspoon vanilla

1¼ cups each, half-and-half and
    milk, scalded
12 blanched almonds (optional)

Place ½ cup sugar in 8-inch layer-cake pan over low heat. Holding pan with potholder, stir with long-handled wooden spoon until sugar melts and is golden brown. Tilt pan to distribute caramel evenly on sides and bottom; set aside. With whisk beat eggs, 3 tablespoons sugar and the vanilla until blended. Gradually add hot milk-cream mixture, beating constantly until blended. Set prepared layer pan in 13 x 9 x 2-inch baking pan; pour custard into layer pan. Place on rack in center of preheated 300°F. oven. Pour hot water to ½-inch depth in baking pan. Bake 25 to 30 minutes or until knife inserted in center comes out clean. Cool on rack, then chill overnight. Run spatula around edge and carefully turn out on serving plate with high rim or in 9-inch pie plate. Garnish with almonds. Cut in wedges. Serves 6.

RICE IMPERIAL

1 cup candied fruit
¼ cup brandy
1 cup uncooked rice
2 cups boiling water
2 cups milk
¼ teaspoon salt

1 envelope unflavored gelatin
4 egg yolks
1 cup sugar
1 teaspoon vanilla
1 cup heavy cream, whipped

Soak fruit overnight in brandy. Cook rice in boiling water about 10 minutes. Pour off water and finish cooking rice in 1⅓ cups milk, to which salt has been added. Put aside to cool. Meanwhile sprinkle gelatin on ⅔ cup cold milk in top part of double boiler. Cook over boiling water, adding egg yolks, sugar and vanilla. Stir constantly and cook until thickened. Mix with rice. Cool. Stir in undrained fruit and then the whipped cream. Chill. Serves 6. **NOTE:** If desired, pour cooled mixture into 1½-quart mold. Chill until firm. Unmold and decorate with cream.

ALMOND CUSTARD

(color plate 4, bottom)

4 eggs
3 teaspoons vanilla, divided
1 teaspoon almond extract
1¼ cups each, milk and half-
  and-half, scalded together

1 can (6 ounces) frozen apple-
  juice concentrate, undiluted
2 tablespoons sliced toasted
  almonds

With whisk or fork beat eggs, 2 teaspoons vanilla and the almond extract just until blended. Gradually beat in hot milk mixture until blended. Pour into well-greased 1-quart shallow baking dish. Place dish in large shallow pan on rack in center of preheated 300°F. oven. Pour ½ inch hot water into pan. Bake 30 to 40 minutes or until knife inserted in center comes out clean. Remove to rack; cool, then chill. Meanwhile cook juice in small saucepan over high heat until juice is reduced to half, about 10 minutes. Stir in remaining 1 teaspoon vanilla; cool. Just before serving, pour over custard and sprinkle with almonds. Serves 6.

LEMON-WINE GELATIN

(color plate 6, right)

1 envelope unflavored gelatin
½ cup sugar
½ cup boiling water
1 teaspoon grated lemon peel
⅓ cup lemon juice

1¼ cups dry white wine
4 strawberries (optional)
4 thin lemon slices (optional)
Lemon Custard Sauce (optional,
  page 154)

In small deep bowl combine gelatin and sugar. Stir in boiling water until gelatin and sugar dissolve. Stir in peel, juice and wine. Chill until mixture is consistency of unbeaten egg white. Beat until foamy. Pour into 4 wineglasses and chill until set. Garnish each with strawberry and lemon slice. Serves 4.

BLENDER CHOCOLATE MOUSSE FOR 1 OR 2

2 squares (1 ounce each)
  semisweet chocolate or ⅓ cup
  semisweet chocolate pieces
1 tablespoon water
1 teaspoon instant coffee

1 egg
1 tablespoon sugar
½ teaspoon vanilla
⅓ cup heavy cream

Place chocolate, water and coffee in small heavy saucepan; stir over very low heat until melted; set aside. In blender whirl egg, sugar and vanilla about 45 seconds or until frothy. Add cream; blend 10 seconds. Add chocolate mixture; blend until smooth. Pour into 2 small dessert cups. Chill until set. **NOTE:** Recipe may be doubled.

CHOCOLATE MOUSSE WITH MOCHA WHIPPED CREAM

1 tablespoon butter or margarine
3 squares (1 ounce each)
   unsweetened chocolate
2 eggs, separated
Dash of salt
½ cup confectioners' sugar,
   divided

1 cup heavy cream
1 teaspoon vanilla or 1
   tablespoon rum
Mocha Whipped Cream II
   (optional, page 150) or
   whipped cream

Melt butter and chocolate in small heavy saucepan over very low heat or in bowl in microwave oven. Stir until smooth; set aside. In small bowl of mixer beat egg whites and salt until foamy. Gradually beat in ¼ cup sugar until stiff peaks form. Add cream; beat until stiff and well blended; set aside. In large bowl of mixer beat egg yolks, remaining ¼ cup sugar and the vanilla until well blended. Fold in chocolate mixture, then gently fold in egg-white mixture just to blend. Spoon into 4 dessert cups. Chill several hours. Just before serving, garnish with Mocha Whipped Cream II.

FUDGE BATTER PUDDING

1 cup flour
1 cup granulated sugar, divided
½ cup chopped nuts
3 tablespoons plus ⅓ cup cocoa,
   divided
2 teaspoons baking powder
½ teaspoon salt

½ cup milk
3 tablespoons butter or
   margarine, melted
1 teaspoon vanilla
1⅔ cups hot water
Confectioners' sugar
Heavy cream, milk or vanilla ice
   cream

In greased deep 2-quart round casserole mix well flour, ½ cup granulated sugar, the nuts, 3 tablespoons cocoa, the baking powder and salt; set aside. Mix milk, butter and vanilla; stir into flour mixture to blend well. Sprinkle evenly with remaining ⅓ cup cocoa and ½ cup granulated sugar. Pour on water. Bake in preheated 350°F. oven 40 minutes or until pick inserted in center of cake comes out clean. Sprinkle with confectioners' sugar. Spoon out at once into dessert dishes, serving some sauce with cake. Pass cream. Serves 6 to 8.

DANISH RUM PUDDING WITH RASPBERRY SAUCE

1 envelope unflavored gelatin
1 cup sugar, divided
¼ teaspoon salt
1¼ cups milk
4 eggs, separated

¼ cup light rum
1 cup heavy cream, whipped
Fresh strawberries (optional)
Raspberry Sauce (page 154)

In top part of double boiler mix gelatin, ½ cup sugar and the salt. Stir in milk and heat to scalding. Beat egg yolks slightly and gradually stir in milk mixture. Put over simmering water and cook, stirring, until mixture coats a metal spoon. Add rum, cool, then chill until mixture begins to set. Beat egg whites until foamy, then gradually add remaining sugar and beat until stiff. Fold with whipped cream into first mixture. Pour into 2-quart mold rinsed with cold water and chill 4 hours or overnight. Unmold and fill center with strawberries, if desired. Serve with the sauce. Serves 8.

CHEESE-PRUNE PUDDING

2 cups cottage cheese	3 eggs
½ cup sour cream	12 ounces pitted prunes,
2 teaspoons vanilla	chopped (2 cups)
½ teaspoon cinnamon or ground	1 cup chopped nuts
cardamom, or to taste	Orange Sauce (page 154) *or* 1 can
¼ teaspoon salt	(8 ounces) crushed pineapple
	in own juice

In large bowl of mixer beat cottage cheese, sour cream, vanilla, cinnamon and salt until well blended. Beat in eggs, one at a time, until well blended. Fold in prunes and nuts. Spoon into greased 2-quart casserole; bake in preheated 300°F. oven 1 hour 15 minutes or until firm. Serve warm or cold, topped with Orange Sauce or pineapple. Serves 8.

RICE PUDDING WITH STRAWBERRY SAUCE

¼ cup uncooked rice	½ cup cold water
4 cups boiling water	1 tablespoon grated lemon rind
2 cups milk	1 cup heavy cream, whipped
½ teaspoon salt	1 pint strawberries, washed and
1 cup sugar	hulled
2 envelopes unflavored gelatin	1 tablespoon lemon juice

Boil rice briskly, uncovered, in the boiling water 2 minutes. Drain and rinse with cold water. Return to saucepan. Add 1 cup milk and the salt. Bring to a boil, cover and simmer 20 minutes. Remove from heat and add remaining milk and ½ cup sugar. Cool. Soften gelatin in the cold water. Dissolve over low heat and add to cooled rice mixture. Chill until thickened but not firm. Add lemon rind and whipped cream. Pour into 1-quart mold rinsed with cold water. Cover and chill overnight. Unmold and pour sauce over top. **To make sauce,** slice strawberries, add remaining ½ cup sugar and the lemon juice. Chill until serving time. Serves 6.

LEMON PUDDING CAKE

3 tablespoons butter or
  margarine, softened
1 cup sugar
4 eggs, separated
3 tablespoons all-purpose flour

¼ teaspoon salt
⅓ cup lemon juice
2 teaspoons grated lemon rind
1 cup milk

Cream butter, gradually add sugar and beat until well blended. Add egg yolks and beat until light and fluffy. Stir in next 4 ingredients, then gradually add milk. Beat whites until stiff, and carefully fold into batter. Pour into shallow 1-quart baking dish and set in pan of hot water. Bake in slow oven (325°F.) 40 minutes. Turn temperature control to 350°F. and bake 10 minutes longer. Serve warm or chilled. Serves 4 to 6.

CRANBERRY PUDDING CAKE

1½ cups cranberries
Sugar
2 teaspoons cornstarch
Butter or margarine
Dash of nutmeg
1 cup plus 2 tablespoons all-
  purpose flour

2 teaspoons baking powder
½ cup milk
½ cup chopped dates
½ cup chopped nuts
½ cup raisins
Heavy cream or ice cream

Put cranberries in saucepan with 1⅓ cups water and cook until berries pop. Mix 1 cup plus 2 tablespoons sugar and the cornstarch and gradually stir into berries. Cook, stirring frequently, 5 minutes. Remove from heat and add 1 tablespoon butter and the nutmeg. Put in greased 8-inch square pan. Mix flour, baking powder and ½ cup sugar. Cut in ¼ cup butter until mixture is the texture of cornmeal. Add milk and mix well. Stir in remaining ingredients, except cream. Drop by tablespoonfuls into hot cranberry mixture and bake in slow oven (325°F.) about 50 minutes. Serve with cream. Serves 8.

OATMEAL-DATE PUDDING CAKE

1½ cups pitted dates, cut up
Sugar
1¼ cups sifted all-purpose flour
2 teaspoons baking powder
½ teaspoon baking soda

¾ teaspoon salt
½ cup quick-cooking rolled oats
¼ cup butter
¾ cup buttermilk

Put dates, ¾ cup sugar and 1 cup water in saucepan, bring to boil and cook, stirring, 10 minutes or until thick. Spread in buttered 8-inch square cake pan. Sift 2 tablespoons sugar and next 4 ingredients into bowl. Add oats and cut in butter. Add buttermilk and mix well. Spread on top of dates and bake in moderate oven (350°F.) 30 minutes. Good warm or cold.

15
FRESH-FRUIT DESSERTS

In the past fresh fruits have often been overlooked as dessert—either they were not always available or, if they were, the eye was so trained to the more spectacular dish that fruit was relegated to a place in the meal just before or after dessert. Today all that has changed. Not only are fresh fruits from around the world available all year, but we have also become much more health-conscious, recognizing that the sweet, fragrant taste of fresh fruit is as satisfying as any other kind of dessert.

As *Woman's Day* readers have discovered, there are many, many ways to serve fruit as dessert—either plain or in simple yet elegant combinations—raw, marinated, baked or stewed. In addition to the recipes here, there is at the end of this chapter a list of appealing ideas for other fruit desserts to use as inspiration as fruits and berries come into season.

SPRING AMBROSIA

½ cup sugar
1 pound rhubarb, cut in
   1-inch pieces (3 cups)

⅔ cup flaked coconut
3 large oranges
1 banana

In saucepan mix sugar and ½ cup water. Bring to boil and add rhubarb. Cover, bring quickly to boil and turn off heat. Let stand, covered, until lukewarm. Pour into bowl and chill. Put coconut on waxed paper. Peel oranges and banana and slice crosswise. In serving dish, overlap orange slices around edge. Spoon rhubarb and banana slices into center and decorate with a ring of coconut. Serves 6. **NOTE:** Sweetened strawberries may be added.

PEACH-BLUEBERRY COMPOTE

5 large peaches, peeled and cut
   in ½-inch slices
1½ cups blueberries, rinsed

Vanilla Syrup (page 155)
About 1 cup heavy cream

Combine peaches and blueberries in a serving bowl. Pour hot syrup with vanilla pod over fruit, cover and chill. At serving time ladle into dessert bowls and pass cream. Serves 6.

VANILLA POACHED PEARS

4 medium pears, halved, peeled
   and cored
Lemon juice
1 cup water

½ to ¾ cup sugar
1 teaspoon vanilla
Vanilla ice cream

Brush pears with lemon juice. In large skillet combine water, sugar and vanilla. Bring to boil, stirring to dissolve sugar. Add pear halves, cut side down. Bring to boil. Cover and simmer, turning pears occasionally, 10 to 25 minutes or until pears are just fork-tender. Serve warm with ice cream. Serves 4.

POIRES GLACÉES
(Stuffed Pears with Apricot Glaze)

*A beautiful, traditional French dessert, gourmet all
the way.*

12 ripe pears
Vanilla Syrup (page 155)
1 can or jar (10½ ounces) whole
   chestnuts in syrup

1 jar (1 pound) apricot preserves
2 tablespoons cognac

Peel pears and remove core from bottom of each pear, leaving a cavity at base. Prepare syrup. Add pears and cook until just tender, spooning syrup over them as they cook. You can poach pears in two or more batches, using the same syrup over again. Drain pears and cool. Break up chestnuts, and when pears are cool, stuff cavities with broken chestnut meats. Arrange on serving dish. Put apricot preserves in small saucepan and bring to boil over medium heat. Add cognac and cook down 3 minutes, stirring. Put preserves through sieve and cool slightly. Spoon or brush over surface of pears. Chill thoroughly and decorate with candied violets and chopped pistachio nuts.

RHUBARB-STRAWBERRY COMPOTE

*Delicious with sweetened whipped cream flavored
with kirsch or vanilla.*

4 cups sliced fresh or frozen
    rhubarb (1 pound)
1 cup sugar
⅛ teaspoon salt

2 cups fresh or thawed frozen
    strawberries, hulled and
    halved (1 pint)
2 medium oranges, peeled, sliced
    and halved (optional)

In large stainless-steel or enamelware skillet mix rhubarb, sugar and salt. Cover and cook over very low heat, without stirring, 20 to 25 minutes or until rhubarb is tender, shaking skillet occasionally. Cool. Stir in strawberries and oranges. Chill in serving dish. Serves 4 to 6.

GINGERED PINEAPPLE COMPOTE

1 large ripe pineapple
2 tablespoons lemon juice
½ cup sugar

1 cup water
½ teaspoon ginger

Cut top from pineapple, then cut in quarters lengthwise. Cut off cores, then cut flesh from peel. Cut each quarter in half lengthwise, then cut crosswise in 1-inch chunks (makes about 4 cups). Place in serving bowl and sprinkle with lemon juice; set aside. In small saucepan stir together sugar, water and ginger; bring to boil and simmer 5 minutes. Pour over pineapple. Chill. Serves 4 to 6. **NOTE:** If desired, use equal amount of canned un-sweetened pineapple chunks, reserving liquid and substituting it for the water.

ALMOND-RAISIN COMPOTE

1 cup each, seedless raisins and
    water
¼ to ½ teaspoon almond extract

2 or 3 each bananas, oranges or
    combination, peeled and
    sliced

Mix well raisins, water and extract. Cover and let stand overnight. Bring to boil, reduce heat, cover and simmer 10 minutes. Serve warm over sliced fruit. Serves 4.

SPICY APPLE COMPOTE

Buy or pick apples at the peak of the season, when they are fresh and juicy, and prepare this delicious dessert for all year round.

1 can (6 ounces) frozen
    cranberry-juice-cocktail
    concentrate
3 juice-cans cold water
1 cup sugar
½ lemon, sliced thin

1 cinnamon stick about 4 inches
    long
6 cloves
8 medium (2½ pounds) firm
    cooking apples, peeled, cored
    and halved

In large saucepan dissolve concentrate in water. Add sugar, lemon, cinnamon stick and cloves. Bring to a boil, stirring to dissolve sugar. Adding 5 or 6 apple halves at a time, simmer in hot syrup, turning halves once, 6 to 8 minutes or until almost tender. Discard lemon, cinnamon and cloves. Chill and serve, or store covered in refrigerator up to 3 weeks. Or pack apples and syrup into hot, sterilized jars. Seal at once. Process in boiling-water bath 20 minutes. Store in cool, dry place. Chill before serving. Serve topped with whipped cream or vanilla ice cream. Also good as a condiment. Makes 16 apple halves.

MARINATED ORANGES

1 or 2 oranges, peeled and sliced
⅓ cup orange liqueur

1 tablespoon sliced almonds
    (optional)

Arrange orange slices in serving dish; pour on liqueur, cover and chill overnight. Sprinkle with almonds just before serving. Serves 1 or 2.

FRESH FRUIT IN YOGURT SAUCE

1 cup plain yogurt
3 tablespoons honey
1 tablespoon frozen orange-juice
    concentrate, thawed
Dash of nutmeg

2 cups cantaloupe chunks
2 cups unpeeled apple chunks
2 cups fresh strawberry halves
2 cups peach or pear chunks

Combine yogurt, honey, concentrate and nutmeg; set aside. In large bowl combine fruits, add yogurt mixture and toss gently. Serve with picks. Makes 2 quarts.

PEARS IN WINE-RASPBERRY SAUCE

1 cup seedless raspberry jam
1 cup rosé wine

6 firm-ripe winter pears, peeled
and cored

Heat jam and wine in skillet. Add pears and poach gently, basting frequently with the mixture, 20 minutes or until pears are tender. Remove from heat, cool, then chill in the mixture. Serves 6.

BAKED PEARS, MARMALADE

½ cup orange marmalade
2 tablespoons packed brown
sugar
1 tablespoon butter or margarine

Dash of cloves
Cinnamon
6 firm-ripe pears, halved and
cored (peeled if desired)
Sour cream

In small saucepan simmer marmalade, sugar, butter, cloves and dash of cinnamon until blended, 2 to 3 minutes. Place pears cut side down in 13 x 9 x 2-inch baking dish and pour syrup over all. Bake in 350°F. oven 30 minutes or until pears are tender and glazed, basting occasionally with syrup. (Time will vary with ripeness of fruit.) Serve warm with sour cream and sprinkling of cinnamon. Serves 6 or 12.

FRUIT PLATE WITH BRANDIED DATE SAUCE

1 cup finely chopped dates
About ¾ cup water
½ cup orange juice
2 tablespoons brandy
1 fresh ripe pineapple, cut into
chunks, or 1 can (15¼ ounces)
pineapple chunks, chilled and
drained

About ½ pint strawberries,
halved
About 1½ cups seeded halved
grapes
1 pound fresh ripe peaches,
sliced, or 1 can (16 ounces)
peach slices, chilled and
drained

In small saucepan bring to boil dates, water and orange juice, then simmer 10 minutes or until dates are very soft. Add more water if necessary, to keep soupy. Remove from heat, stir in brandy and chill. Makes 1½ cups sauce. To serve, place sauce in small dish and center on medium platter. Arrange fruits around sauce. Serves 6. **NOTE:** Sauce is delicious on ice cream, custard and unfrosted cake.

OTHER EASY FRUIT DESSERTS

• Serve fragile summer fruits (peaches, cherries, plums, grapes) European fashion. Immerse fruits in cool, not iced, water in pretty glass bowl. The water lightly cools fruits to a refreshing degree without flavor loss and removes surface dust.

• Serve the simplest of all desserts—fresh fruits, your favorite cheese, French or Italian bread and a dry red or dessert wine. Fruits and cheese have fuller flavor if served at room temperature.

• Combine equal amounts diced fruit or berries and plain or vanilla yogurt. Sweeten if desired.

• Sweeten blueberries, sliced peaches or halved green seedless grapes with maple or maple-flavored syrup. Top with sour cream. Sprinkle with cinnamon.

• In blender whirl until smooth 1 cup sliced peaches and ¼ cup orange juice. Add honey or brown sugar. Serve over vanilla ice cream or orange or lemon sherbet.

• Top papaya slices or wedges with vanilla ice cream. Sprinkle with chopped macadamia nuts.

• Poach sliced pitted plums in hot tea flavored with lemon slices and a cinnamon stick. Sweeten to taste and chill.

• Serve melon balls in attractive dessert glasses. Pour on carbonated grapefruit beverage. Garnish with mint.

• Sprinkle sliced peaches or nectarines with sweet sauterne, then with coconut.

• Fold berries into sweetened whipped cream. Delicious filling for cream puffs.

• Combine cantaloupe balls, blueberries and kirsch.

• Flavor vanilla yogurt with frozen orange-juice concentrate or orange liqueur. Serve over raspberries.

• Serve sweetened strawberries or raspberries over orange sherbet; sprinkle with pistachio nuts.

16
FROZEN DESSERTS

This chapter includes homemade ice cream, sherbets, ices, frozen yogurt and a spectacular selection of molded bombes, mousses, soufflés and other frozen concoctions.
Choose desserts in the first four categories to serve plain or with the toppings, sauces or garnishes offered in chapter 19. And you need not stop there. Tube cakes, sponge cakes, cake rolls, cream puffs and crêpes can all be filled, layered or topped with frozen creams and ices. These comprise a whole separate category of glorious frozen desserts—yours to combine and create.

Ice Cream

SUPER-EASY LEMON ICE CREAM WITH COCONUT

2 cups half-and-half
¾ cup sugar
2 tablespoons grated lemon peel

⅓ cup lemon juice (2 large lemons)
¼ cup toasted shredded coconut (page 9)

In mixing bowl stir half-and-half and sugar until sugar is dissolved. Stir in lemon peel and juice. Pour into 9-inch pie pan or divide among 6 sherbet glasses. Beat semifrozen mixture until fluffy. Freeze until firm. Sprinkle with coconut. Serves 6. **NOTE:** If desired, substitute sliced sweetened strawberries for coconut.

Below are two excellent, and very different, recipes for peach ice cream, one made in a crank-type freezer and one in a metal pan.

PEACH ICE CREAM

Make in crank-type freezer

6 egg yolks
2 cups milk
1 cup sugar
¼ teaspoon salt
2 cups heavy cream

1 teaspoon almond extract
2 cups sweetened crushed fresh peaches or thawed frozen peaches

In top part of double boiler beat first 2 ingredients with rotary beater. Add sugar and salt and cook over simmering water, stirring, until mixture thickens and coats a metal spoon. Cool, then add cream and flavoring. Partially freeze in crank-type freezer, then add peaches and finish freezing. Makes about 1¾ quarts.

BLENDER PEACH ICE CREAM

1½ pounds peaches (about 7 medium)
2 tablespoons lemon juice
½ cup each, sugar and light corn syrup

¼ teaspoon almond extract (optional)
⅛ teaspoon salt
1 cup sour cream

Slice peaches into blender or food processor. Add juice, sugar, syrup, extract and salt. Whirl until puréed. Add sour cream and whirl until smooth. Pour into 8-inch square metal pan. Freeze uncovered about 2 hours or until set at edges. Turn into medium bowl. Beat until smooth. Return to pan, cover airtight and freeze until firm. Serves 8.

APRICOT-BRANDY ICE CREAM

Buy or make your own peach ice cream to create this distinctive and unusually pleasing dessert.

1 package (10 ounces) frozen or 1 pound fresh peaches
2 tablespoons sugar (optional)

1 pint peach ice cream
3 ounces (6 tablespoons) apricot brandy

Whirl thawed peaches in blender. If fresh peaches are used, peel, slice and add sugar; whirl in blender. Combine peach purée with softened ice cream and stir in brandy. Work quickly, especially if fruit is not cold. Refreeze in bowl or parfait glasses. Serves 4.

STRAWBERRY ICE CREAM

As pure and delicious as any ice cream could be.

1 quart strawberries (or more to taste)
¾ cup sugar

¼ teaspoon salt
2 cups light cream

Wash and hull berries. Mash well and stir in sugar. Let stand 20 minutes, then force through sieve to remove seeds. Mix with salt and cream and pour into container of crank freezer. Freeze with ice and salt until firm. Makes 1½ quarts. **NOTE:** Two boxes (10 ounces each) frozen sliced strawberries, thawed, can be substituted for the fresh. Stir in ½ cup sugar and force through sieve. Proceed as directed.

ORANGE VELVET ICE CREAM

This is made in a crank-type freezer. For a real treat, use fresh oranges.

2 egg yolks
1 cup light cream
¼ teaspoon salt
2 cups sugar

2 cups orange juice
1 cup heavy cream, whipped
¼ cup finely cut candied orange peel

In top part of small double boiler beat first 3 ingredients together with rotary beater. Put over simmering water and cook, stirring, until mixture is slightly thickened and coats a metal spoon; cool. Boil sugar, 1 cup water and orange juice 5 minutes; cool. Combine mixtures and fold in cream. Partially freeze in crank-type freezer, then add orange peel and freeze. Makes 2 quarts.

LIME ICE CREAM

(color plate 6, bottom left)
Whether or not this is served in a melon shell, it makes a perfect summer dessert.

2 cups heavy cream or half-and-half (see Note)
½ cup each sugar and light corn syrup
1 tablespoon grated lime peel
⅓ cup lime juice

Half honeydew shell, pulp scooped out for other use (optional)
Mint sprigs or thin strips lime peel (optional)
Fresh strawberries (optional)

In 9 x 5 x 3-inch metal loaf pan stir cream, sugar, syrup, peel and juice until sugar dissolves. Cover airtight and freeze until firm, several hours or overnight. Serve from chilled honeydew shell. Garnish with mint sprigs; serve with a strawberry. Makes about 3 cups, or serves 6. **NOTE:** For smoother ice cream, when using half-and-half beat semifrozen mixture until fluffy; refreeze.

PUMPKIN-GINGER ICE CREAM

The spicy flavor we have associated with pumpkin pie
over the years is equally good in this unusual dessert.
It begins like a pumpkin-pie filling.

1 cup sugar
4 egg yolks, slightly beaten
1 teaspoon ground ginger
2 teaspoons vanilla
½ teaspoon cinnamon
¼ teaspoon salt

1½ cups light cream or half-and-half, heated
1 cup cooked pumpkin
2 cups heavy cream
½ cup minced preserved or candied ginger

In top of double boiler combine sugar, egg yolks, ginger, vanilla, cinnamon and salt; blend in light cream. Cook over hot, *not boiling*, water about 5 minutes or until mixture coats spoon, stirring constantly (do not overcook). Blend well with pumpkin; cool. Add heavy cream and mix well. Following manufacturer's directions, freeze mixture half at a time in electric ice cream maker 30 minutes. Stop machine, remove ice cream and add half the ginger. Continue freezing until done. Pack ice cream into tightly covered freezer container for storage. Repeat procedure with remaining ice cream mixture. Set freezer at coldest setting. Makes 2 quarts. **NOTE:** If preferred, freeze in mold or ice cream trays, but *whip heavy cream stiff before folding into other ingredients.*

"ICED-COFFEE" DESSERT

If desired, substitute one cup toasted fresh coconut
(page 9) for canned.

1 envelope unflavored gelatin
¾ cup milk
⅔ cup sugar
¼ teaspoon salt

2½ tablespoons instant coffee (not freeze-dried)
2 cups heavy cream
1 can (4½ ounces) toasted coconut

Sprinkle gelatin on milk in small saucepan and let stand 5 minutes to soften. Add sugar and salt and heat, stirring, until gelatin and sugar dissolve. Chill until slightly thickened. Combine coffee with cream and whip until stiff. Thoroughly fold cream and most of coconut (save some for decoration) into gelatin mixture. Spoon into dessert dishes and freeze until firm. Serve slightly thawed with a sprinkling of coconut. Serves 10 to 12.

RICH BANANA ICE CREAM

Luscious as is or with a sprinkling of finely chopped walnuts.

2 eggs
½ cup sugar
Dash of salt
1½ cups thinly sliced *very ripe* bananas (2 medium)

2 teaspoons lemon juice
½ teaspoon vanilla
½ cup light corn syrup
1½ cups heavy cream
½ cup milk

In large bowl of mixer beat eggs, sugar and salt until thick and light-colored; set aside. Beat bananas, lemon juice and vanilla until very smooth; beat into egg mixture. Beat in syrup, cream and milk until well blended. Freeze until almost firm. Beat until smooth. Freeze again, then beat again. Turn into chilled 9 x 9-inch baking pan or 9 x 5 x 3-inch loaf pan. Freeze until firm, then cover airtight. Makes about 5 cups, or serves 8.

DOUBLE-CHOCOLATE ICE CREAM

Extra-rich and sinfully delicious.

½ cup sugar
1 tablespoon flour
⅛ teaspoon salt
2 eggs
1 cup half-and-half or milk
3 squares (1 ounce each) unsweetened chocolate, melted

2 teaspoons vanilla
1 cup heavy cream
3 squares (1 ounce each) semisweet chocolate, chopped coarse (in blender, food processor or with sharp knife)

Place sugar, flour, salt and eggs in heavy saucepan. Beat with wooden spoon until blended. Beat in half-and-half. Stir over low heat until mixture coats spoon and is smooth (*do not overcook*). Add melted chocolate and vanilla; beat until well blended and smooth; cool. Whip cream; fold into chocolate mixture to blend. Fold in chopped chocolate. Pour into chilled loaf pan, cover airtight and freeze. Let stand at room temperature 15 minutes before serving. Makes about 3 cups, or serves 6. **NOTE:** To make ice cream in electric ice cream maker *do not whip cream*. Follow manufacturer's directions, setting freezer at coldest setting.

Ices, Sherbets and Frozen Yogurts

These light and soothing desserts are the perfect antidote for summer's heat and are usually low in calories as well. Many fruits lend themselves to all three categories, equally delicious but distinctly different.

FRESH-STRAWBERRY ICE

Omit brandy, if desired.

4 cups thinly sliced hulled ripe strawberries
About 1 cup sugar

2 tablespoons brandy
1 teaspoon lemon juice

Toss berries with sugar. Let stand at room temperature until sugar dissolves and juices form, about 30 minutes. Add brandy and lemon juice. Whirl in blender until smooth. Pour into large bowl of mixer; freeze until almost firm. Beat until smooth. Freeze again, then beat again. Spread in chilled shallow 8 x 8-inch metal pan or 2 ice trays. Freeze until firm. Cover airtight. Makes about 3 cups, or serves 6.

WINTER VARIATION

2 packages (10 ounces each) frozen sweetened strawberries, partially thawed

3 tablespoons sugar
2 tablespoons brandy
1 teaspoon lemon juice

In blender whirl until smooth strawberries, sugar, brandy, lemon juice. Freeze and beat as above. Makes about 3 cups, or serves 6.

TART LIME ICE

Garnish with just a lime slice.

1 cup sugar
2 cups water

1 tablespoon grated lime peel
⅔ cup lime juice

In saucepan boil sugar and water 5 minutes; cool. Pour into large bowl of mixer and stir in lime peel and juice. Freeze until mushy. Beat until smooth. Freeze again, then beat again. Spread in chilled shallow 8 x 8-inch metal pan or 2 ice trays. Freeze until firm. Cover airtight. Makes about 3 cups, or serves 6.

WINE ICE WITH PINEAPPLE AND STRAWBERRIES

This makes a beautiful presentation on a hot summer day.
Make Wine Ice the day before serving.

½ cup granulated sugar
1 teaspoon grated lemon rind
2 to 3 tablespoons lemon juice
2 cups semidry white wine
1 small very ripe pineapple, cut
   in chunks

Sliced fresh strawberries or
   frozen raspberries, almost
   thawed
Confectioners' sugar (optional)
Whipped cream (optional)

Combine granulated sugar with 1 cup water in small saucepan. Bring to boil, stirring, then cool. Add lemon rind, juice and wine. Pour into 3-cup mold or plastic container, preferably with rounded bottom, and freeze overnight, stirring twice after mixture begins to get mushy. Before serving, dip mold or container in warm water. When loosened, unmold on chilled platter. Arrange fruit around mold and let stand at room temperature 10 minutes before serving. Pass confectioners' sugar and whipped cream if desired. Serves 6 to 8. **NOTE:** Other fruits, such as cherries, halved and pitted blue grapes, mandarin oranges, frozen strawberries or canned apricots, can also be used.

FRESH-STRAWBERRY SHERBET

1 quart ripe strawberries
1 cup sugar
Dash of salt

Juice of 1 lemon
Juice of 1 orange
2 egg whites

Wash berries and remove caps. Crush with sugar; let stand ½ hour. Add 1 cup water and heat to boiling. Strain through a fine sieve. Chill. Add remaining ingredients, put in crank-type freezer and freeze until firm. Makes about 1¼ quarts.

WATERMELON ICE

¼ large watermelon
1 envelope unflavored gelatin
Juice of 1 lemon

½ cup sugar
⅛ teaspoon salt

Remove seeds from melon and whirl pink meat in blender. Strain (you will need 3 cups melon juice). Soften gelatin in ¼ cup juice in small saucepan and dissolve over low heat or hot water. Add with lemon juice, sugar and salt to remaining watermelon juice. Put in crank-type freezer and freeze until of sherbet consistency. Makes about 1 quart.

FRESH-PEACH ICE

1 cup sugar
2½ cups water

2½ cups peeled and sliced ripe
   white or golden peaches
1½ to 2 teaspoons lemon juice

In medium saucepan boil sugar and water 5 minutes; cool. Add peaches and lemon juice. Whirl in blender until smooth. Pour into large bowl of mixer and freeze until mushy. Beat until smooth. Freeze again, then beat again. Spread in chilled shallow 8 x 8-inch metal pan or 2 ice trays. Freeze until firm. Cover airtight. Makes about 1 quart, or serves 8.

WINTER VARIATION

1 can (29 ounces) sliced peaches
   in syrup

3 tablespoons sugar
1½ teaspoons lemon juice

Drain peaches, reserving ⅔ cup syrup. Whirl peaches, reserved syrup, sugar and lemon juice in blender until smooth. Freeze and beat as above. Makes 3½ cups, or serves 6 or 7.

PEACH SHERBET

1 cup sugar
2 cups fresh-peach pulp (see
   Note)

½ cup each, orange and lemon
   juices
1 egg white
⅛ teaspoon salt

Boil sugar and 1 cup water together 5 minutes. Cool. Mix all ingredients. Put in crank-type freezer and freeze until firm. Makes about 1¼ quarts. **NOTE:** To make peach pulp, pit soft ripe peaches and press through sieve or food mill or whirl in blender.

FRESH-RASPBERRY SHERBET

Homemade, there is no equal.

1 quart red raspberries
1 cup sugar
Dash of salt

Juice of 1 lemon
Juice of 1 orange
2 egg whites

Wash berries; crush with sugar and 1 cup water. Let stand 10 minutes. Heat to boiling and strain through fine cloth. Chill. Add remaining ingredients, put in crank-type freezer and freeze until firm. Makes about 1¼ quarts.

CRANBERRY SHERBET

1 pound cranberries
1¼ cups sugar or more, to taste
1 cup orange juice
Juice of 1 lemon

Grated rind of 1 orange
Dash of salt
2 egg whites, stiffly beaten

Cook cranberries with 2 cups water 10 minutes. Force through coarse sieve. Add enough water to pulp and juice to make 2 cups. Add sugar to hot mixture, then add orange and lemon juices, grated rind and salt. Fold in egg whites. Put in crank-type freezer and freeze until firm. Makes about 1¼ quarts.

NECTARINE SHERBET

Yogurt gives this sherbet its creamy flavor.

1 container (8 ounces) plain
   yogurt
2 cups thinly sliced nectarines

½ cup honey
½ cup orange juice
Nectarine or Peach Sauce (page
   154)

Put all ingredients except sauce in blender. Whirl until well blended, pour into 2 refrigerator trays and freeze until firm around edges. Turn into chilled bowl and beat until smooth. Put back in trays and freeze until set. Let stand at room temperature 10 minutes before spooning into 6 individual dishes. Serve topped with sauce if desired. Serves 6.

FROZEN BANANA YOGURT

1 envelope unflavored gelatin
¼ cup cold water
½ cup sugar
¼ teaspoon salt
1 cup mashed ripe bananas
   (about 3)

1 tablespoon lemon juice
1 container (8 ounces) plain
   yogurt
2 egg whites, unbeaten

In small saucepan sprinkle gelatin over water. Stir over low heat until gelatin dissolves, about 3 minutes. Stir in sugar and salt. Remove from heat; stir in bananas and lemon juice, then yogurt. Pour into freezer tray or 9 x 5 x 3-inch loaf pan. Freeze until firm. Turn mixture into large bowl of mixer, let soften slightly, then add egg whites. Beat at high speed until smooth and fluffy, about 10 minutes. Freeze in tray until firm. Makes 6 cups.

SHERBET IN PINEAPPLE SHELL

Freeze the sherbet in the hollow pineapple shell for an attractive presentation.

1 medium-size ripe pineapple	1 tablespoon lemon juice
1 cup water	

To make shell and remove pulp, cut off crown about 2 inches from top of pineapple; set aside. Holding pineapple upright, with long, sharp knife cut around pulp close to rind (don't pierce, or it will leak). Remove pulp, slice, discard tough center core, then dice pulp. Refrigerate shell and crown. In medium saucepan mix diced pulp (about 1 cup), water and lemon juice. Cook over moderate heat about 5 minutes. Purée in food processor or blender. Freeze in freezer tray until firm but not hard. Beat until fluffy. Spoon into pineapple shell. Freeze until firm. Makes about 2 cups, or serves 4.

FRESH-MINT SHERBET

1 envelope unflavored gelatin	⅔ cup lemon juice
1 cup sugar	2 tablespoons minced fresh mint
4¼ cups water, divided	

In medium saucepan mix gelatin and sugar; add 1 cup water and stir over low heat until dissolved, about 5 minutes. Remove from heat and stir in remaining 3¼ cups water, the lemon juice and mint. Turn into freezer container and freeze until slushy; beat until foamy. Return to freezer and repeat procedure once more, then freeze until firm. Makes 1 quart.

STRAWBERRY-YOGURT FREEZE

1 cup plain yogurt	⅓ cup honey
2 cups fresh strawberries, halved	1 tablespoon lemon juice

Whirl all ingredients in blender until smooth. Pour into ice-cube tray and freeze until firm around edges. Turn into chilled bowl and beat until smooth. Put back in tray and freeze until firm. Let stand at room temperature to soften slightly before serving. Makes 2¾ cups. **NOTE:** If desired, 2 cups sliced fresh peaches can be substituted for berries.

FROZEN PEACH YOGURT

(color plate 5, top)
Make in ice-cream maker or freezer.

1⅓ cups sliced soft ripe peaches	**⅛ teaspoon almond extract**
½ cup sugar	**2 cups plain yogurt**
Dash of salt	

In blender or food processor coarsely purée peaches (1 cup). Mix with sugar, salt and extract. Stir in yogurt just to blend. Turn mixture into can of electric ice-cream maker (no more than two thirds full). Insert dasher, cover and follow manufacturer's directions for use. When very thick (25 to 90 minutes, depending on ice-cream maker), turn into 9-inch square pan or tray container, cover airtight and ripen in freezer about 2 hours. Remove from freezer 15 to 20 minutes before serving. Makes about 1 quart, or serves 6.

FREEZER VERSION Turn yogurt mixture into 9-inch square pan. Freeze until set at edges, about 1 hour. Turn into large bowl of mixer and beat at low speed until smooth. Return to tray and freeze until firm. Cover airtight. Volume is slightly less than that of frozen yogurt prepared in electric maker.

Bombes, Mousses, Soufflés and Other Frozen Concoctions

This section also includes several frozen cakes, pies and tarts too good to ignore.

ICE CREAM BOMBE

A bombe (French for "ball") is a mold consisting of two frozen mixtures—one to line the mold, the other to fill it.

Chill a 1- or 1½-quart dome-shaped mold or mixing bowl. (If using a mixing bowl, place two 18 x 2-inch strips of foil crosswise in bowl, letting ends hang over. They will help to unmold ice cream later.) Fill with slightly softened ice cream, spreading on bottom and sides to each 1-inch thickness. Fill center with second mixture. (See suggestions at ending.)

Cover with waxed paper, pressing with hand to smooth top. Freeze overnight or longer. To unmold ice cream, dip mold in cool water. Invert on chilled plate, pulling ends of foil to help remove ice cream. Put back in freezer until serving time. Garnish with whipped cream and a sprinkle of chopped pistachio nuts. Slice or cut in wedges. **NOTE:** Because ice cream packs down, you will need about 2 quarts for 1½-quart mold—1½ quarts ice cream to line mold and 1 pint to fill it.

SUGGESTED FILLING COMBINATIONS
Pistachio ice cream with raspberry-sherbet center.
Peach ice cream with lemon-sherbet center.
Vanilla ice cream with orange-sherbet center.
Strawberry ice cream with pineapple-sherbet center.
Peppermint ice cream with chocolate ice cream center.

VANILLA-STRAWBERRY BOMBE

(color plate 3, bottom)

2 pints strawberries, hulled, or 2 bags (16 ounces each) frozen unsweetened whole strawberries, thawed and divided

Sugar
2 to 3 pints vanilla ice cream, slightly softened

Chill well a 1- to 1½-quart melon- or dome-shaped mold or mixing bowl. (If using mixing bowl, place two 18 x 2-inch strips of foil or waxed paper crosswise in bowl, extending ends over rim, to help with unmolding.) In blender or food processor purée 1 pint strawberries. Pour into 9-inch square pan. Stir in ⅓ to ½ cup sugar, depending on sweetness of berries; mix well. Freeze until mushy. Meanwhile, working quickly, pack ice cream on bottom and sides of mold or bowl to form 1-inch shell. Freeze about 15 minutes to harden. Stir partially frozen strawberry mixture and fill center of lined mold. Cover tight and freeze overnight or longer. To unmold, dip mold in cool water or wrap in hot dish towel. Invert onto chilled plate and tap mold gently. (If using bowl, pull ends of foil to help remove ice cream.) Place in freezer until serving time. Meanwhile slice and sweeten to taste the remaining 1 pint berries. (If desired, reserve a few whole berries for garnish.) Let sliced berries stand at room temperature 30 minutes, stirring occasionally. To serve, slice bombe or cut in wedges and serve with sweetened berries. Serves 8 to 10.
VANILLA-BLUEBERRY BOMBE Substitute 2 pints blueberries or 2 packages (16 ounces each) unsweetened frozen blueberries for the strawberries. Flavor puréed blueberries with 1 teaspoon lemon juice and dash of salt.

TORTONI

*As simple as can be; use your own homemade vanilla,
or a rich store-bought, ice cream.*

1 pint vanilla ice cream,
softened
¼ cup finely chopped candied
fruit

¼ cup salted almonds, chopped
6 whole salted almonds
(optional)

Mix well ice cream, fruit and chopped almonds without allowing ice cream to melt. Spoon into 6 lightly greased or paper-lined muffin cups. Top each with whole almond. Cover and freeze. Serves 6.

COFFEE-ALMOND TORTONI

*This is also an Italian treat, frozen in paper baking
cups.*

1 egg white
2 tablespoons plus ¼ cup sugar
1 cup heavy cream
1 tablespoon instant coffee
1 teaspoon vanilla

⅛ teaspoon almond extract
½ cup toasted slivered almonds
8 maraschino cherries, drained
(optional)

In small bowl of mixer beat egg white at medium speed until foamy. Gradually add 2 tablespoons sugar and beat at high speed until stiff peaks form. Add cream, ¼ cup sugar, the coffee, vanilla and almond extract; beat until stiff and well blended. Fold in ⅓ cup almonds. Spoon high in eight 2½-inch paper baking cups (in muffin pan, if desired). Sprinkle with remaining almonds. Freeze until firm. Garnish each with cherry. Serves 8.

SPUMONI

This is one of Italy's most popular desserts.

LIGHT PORTION:

2 egg yolks
2 tablespoons sugar

¼ cup marsala wine (or any
other sweet white wine)
½ cup heavy cream

Beat egg yolks with 1 tablespoon water, the sugar and wine. Then transfer to double boiler and continue beating with spoon over simmering water until mixture thickens. Remove from heat. While mixture is cooling, beat cream until it forms stiff peaks. When egg-yolk mixture is cool, fold in cream and transfer to 9 x 5 x 3-inch loaf pan or 2 individual molds and put in freezer.

CHOCOLATE PORTION:

3 tablespoons sugar
1 egg
1 teaspoon flour
¼ cup milk

1 square semisweet chocolate, melted
½ cup heavy cream

While light portion is freezing, prepare chocolate portion. Mix first 4 ingredients together and beat well. Then add the chocolate and stir. Beat cream until stiff; fold into chocolate mixture. When light portion is firm, pour chocolate mixture on top and put back in freezer. To serve, dip pan or mold in hot water a few seconds to loosen. Turn out onto serving dish.

FROZEN RASPBERRY-NUT ROLL

An absolutely stunning summer dessert.

2 boxes (10 ounces each) frozen raspberries, thawed
¾ cup sugar (divided)
2 teaspoons unflavored gelatin
¼ teaspoon almond extract

¾ cup heavy cream, whipped
¼ cup finely chopped nuts (walnuts, pecans, pistachios or blanched almonds)
Fresh-mint sprigs (optional)

Purée berries by forcing through sieve, or purée in blender, then strain. Add ½ cup sugar and enough cold water to make 3 cups mixture. Soften gelatin in ¼ cup water, then dissolve over hot water. Stir into berry mixture. Pour into 2 refrigerator trays and freeze 1½ hours or until mushy. Turn into mixing bowl and beat well. Pour mixture into a lightly oiled 45-ounce juice can (mixture will not fill can). Put in freezer and push solidified mixture into sides of can every ½ hour, leaving center hollow. This will take 1½ to 2 hours. Meanwhile add remaining sugar and the almond extract to cream and beat until stiff. Fold in nuts. Pour into center, cover can with waxed paper and freeze. To unmold, remove bottom, run a spatula around inside of can, then wrap can in hot cloth until dessert slides out. Cut in ¾-inch thick slices, and decorate with mint sprigs if desired. Serves 6 to 8.

STRAWBERRY-ICE ALMOND ROLL

1 quart strawberries
½ cup sugar
½ cup water

1 tablespoon lemon juice
Almond Filling

Wash and hull berries. Purée in blender. Boil sugar and water together about 3 minutes. Cool; combine with berry purée and lemon juice. Pour into pan and freeze, stirring occasionally, until mushy. Turn into mixing bowl and beat well. Put in empty #2½ (about 30 ounces) fruit or vegetable can and freeze until almost firm. Hollow out center of can, packing ice onto sides of can. Fill with Almond Filling, cover and freeze. To serve, wrap outside of can in hot cloth a few seconds, then open other end of can and push through. Slice and serve. Serves 6.
ALMOND FILLING Whip ½ cup heavy cream until stiff. Fold in 3 tablespoons sugar, 3 tablespoons chopped blanched almonds and ¼ teaspoon almond extract.

FROZEN MOCHA SOUFFLÉ

Impressive—can be either frozen or chilled.

8 eggs, separated
¾ cup granulated sugar
2 envelopes unflavored gelatin
½ cup cold strong coffee
¼ cup coffee liqueur or cold
   strong coffee
1 package (4 ounces) sweet
   cooking chocolate, melted

2 ounces unsweetened chocolate,
   melted
2 tablespoons confectioners'
   sugar
2 cups heavy cream
Decorations (see below)

Cut off a piece of waxed paper long enough to go around a 6½-inch to 7-inch 1½- to 2-quart soufflé dish. Fold paper double lengthwise and brush with vegetable oil. Fold around soufflé dish, extending collar 2 to 3 inches above rim. Tie with string and set aside. Beat egg yolks until lemon-colored. Add granulated sugar and beat until light and fluffy. Meanwhile soften gelatin in the coffee and dissolve over low heat. Add to egg mixture with coffee liqueur and chocolates, beating until well blended. Beat egg whites until stiff and fold into first mixture. Combine confectioners' sugar and heavy cream and beat until fluffy. Fold into chocolate mixture. Pour into soufflé dish and freeze 3 to 4 hours or until set and thoroughly chilled. Peel off paper and decorate with ½ cup heavy cream, whipped and mixed with 1 to 2 teaspoons chocolate syrup, and chocolate-covered coffee-bean candies or Chocolate Curls (page 155). Good with strong coffee served in small cups. Serves 10 to 12. **NOTE:** Soufflé can also be refrigerated until set.

FROZEN CHOCOLATE-PECAN MOUSSE RING

(color plate 8, top)

2 eggs, separated
¼ teaspoon salt
½ cup sugar
1 teaspoon vanilla
1 cup heavy cream, whipped
¾ cup toasted chopped pecans

1 square (1 ounce) unsweetened
  chocolate, chopped fine
2 teaspoons oil
3 squares (1 ounce each)
  semisweet chocolate, melted

In small bowl of mixer at medium speed beat egg whites and salt until soft peaks form. Gradually beat in sugar until mixture is glossy and stiff peaks form; set aside. In large bowl beat egg yolks and vanilla with fork until well blended. Fold in about ⅓ egg-white mixture until well blended. Add remaining egg-white mixture, cream, pecans and chopped chocolate; fold to blend well. Line 4-cup ring mold or mixing bowl with plastic wrap. Fill with mixture; smooth top; cover and freeze until firm (or overnight). Blend oil into melted chocolate. Cool. Run small spatula around tube in ring mold. Invert mousse on chilled serving plate. Peel off plastic wrap. Drizzle chocolate-oil mixture over mousse. Return to freezer until serving time. Before serving, decorate with pecan halves if desired. Serves 8.

FROZEN PUMPKIN MOUSSE

Positively the most elegant pumpkin dessert possible.

4 egg yolks
¼ teaspoon salt
1½ cups sugar
1 can (1 pound) pumpkin
Finely cut crystallized ginger
1 teaspoon cinnamon

¼ teaspoon ground cloves
½ teaspoon mace
¼ teaspoon nutmeg
½ cup cognac or bourbon
Heavy cream

Beat egg yolks and salt until thick. Dissolve sugar in ½ cup water in saucepan, bring to boil and boil rapidly until syrup spins a thread—about 230°F. on candy thermometer. Rapidly beat syrup into egg-yolk mixture and continue beating until it begins to cool. This is best done in an electric mixer at high speed. When slightly cooled, combine with pumpkin, ¼ cup ginger, other spices and cognac. Taste for spice. Whip 2 cups cream and fold into mixture. Pour into 2-quart mold or 2 smaller molds of any design or shape, cover and freeze 6 to 8 hours. To unmold, place in refrigerator 20 to 30 minutes, then dip in hot water. Turn out on serving dish. Put back in freezer several minutes, then decorate with whipped cream and ginger and put in freezer 30 minutes before serving. Serves 8 to 10.

FROZEN COFFEE PARFAIT IN MERINGUE

*Make this frozen dessert a day ahead of serving. Allow
at least 3 hours to bake and dry meringues before
assembling. (Three pints quality coffee ice cream may
be substituted for Coffee Parfait.)*

Coffee Parfait (recipe follows)
Meringue Layers (recipe follows)
Whole or halved strawberries

COFFEE PARFAIT *If desired, this delicious parfait can be frozen in individual
parfait glasses and served alone, with berries and whipped cream.*

3 eggs
⅛ teaspoon salt
¾ cup sugar
6 tablespoons water
1½ tablespoons instant espresso-
   coffee powder or crushed
   instant-coffee crystals

¾ teaspoon vanilla
¼ teaspoon lemon juice
1½ cups heavy cream

In large bowl of mixer beat eggs and salt until light and fluffy; set aside. In small heavy
saucepan cook and stir sugar and water until sugar dissolves, then boil *without stirring*
to thread stage (230°F. on candy thermometer). Pour hot syrup in fine stream into beaten
eggs, beating constantly. Turn into top of double boiler; stir over simmering *(not boiling)*
water until mixture is thick and smooth and increased in volume, about 5 minutes. Remove
from heat and stir in coffee powder. Set pan with mixture into bowl of cold water; stir
until cool. Stir in vanilla and lemon juice. Whip cream; fold into mixture. Makes 6 cups.
If served alone, serves 8 to 10.

MERINGUE LAYERS

3 egg whites
¼ teaspoon cream of tartar
6 tablespoons sugar

¾ teaspoon vanilla
3 tablespoons sugar

With finger draw two 7½-inch circles on greased cookie sheet dusted with flour. Beat 3
egg whites and ¼ teaspoon cream of tartar until soft peaks form. Gradually beat in 6
tablespoons sugar and ¾ teaspoon vanilla; beat until stiff but glossy, about 1 minute. Fold
in 3 tablespoons sugar. Spread half the mixture evenly in each circle on cookie sheet. Bake
in 250°F. oven 1 hour. Turn off heat; let cool and dry in oven 2 hours.

Place a Meringue Layer in bottom of 8-inch springform pan, trimming meringue slightly
if necessary, or place in 8-inch layer-cake pan lined with waxed paper that extends above

pan rim. Pour Coffee Parfait over meringue. Top with second Meringue Layer. Freeze until firm. Cover airtight. At serving time loosen edges with thin-bladed knife; remove pan sides. (Or grasp waxed paper and lift out dessert; peel paper from bottom layer.) Place on serving plate. Cut in wedges. Serve with berries. Serves 10.

MERINGUE RING WITH STRAWBERRY ICE CREAM AND STRAWBERRIES

2 pints fresh strawberries
Confectioners' sugar
2 tablespoons sliced pistachio
   nuts
5 egg whites at room
   temperature

¼ teaspoon salt
½ teaspoon cream of tartar
1¾ cups granulated sugar
1 quart strawberry ice cream

Wash and hull berries. Reserve a few whole ones for decoration and slice remainder. Sweeten with confectioners' sugar to taste. Preheat oven to 425°F. Butter a 6-cup ring mold well and sprinkle nuts on bottom; set aside. Beat egg whites with salt and cream of tartar until foamy. Gradually add granulated sugar and beat until stiff, glossy peaks form. Spoon into mold and smooth top with spatula. Tap mold a few times against board to eliminate air bubbles. Put on rack set in center of oven. Turn off heat and leave in oven overnight (do not open oven). Just before serving, unmold on serving platter and fill center with ice cream. Decorate with reserved whole berries and serve with sliced berries. Serves 8.

FROZEN LIME-SHERBET CAKE

(color plate 5, bottom)

This couldn't be easier—and it should inspire any number of new flavor combinations.

1 angel-food cake (12 to 13
   ounces), purchased or home-
   baked, frozen
2 pints lime or other sherbet,
   very slightly softened, divided

Whipped cream or whipped
   topping (optional)
Mint sprigs (optional)

Insert picks midpoint at several places around outside of cake. Using picks as guides, split cake with serrated knife or long thread. With narrow spatula quickly spread 1 pint sherbet on bottom layer. Then quickly spread remaining 1 pint sherbet on top layer, swirling attractively. Carefully place on bottom layer; freeze until surface is hardened. Cover airtight and freeze until firm. Remove from freezer 10 to 15 minutes before serving. Garnish with rosettes or dollops of whipped cream and with mint. If desired, serve with pineapple. Serves 10 to 12.

FROZEN ICE CREAM-PUMPKIN PIE

*An absolutely first-rate alternative to the traditional
pumpkin-pie dessert.*

1½ cups canned pumpkin
½ cup packed light-brown sugar
⅓ cup milk
1 teaspoon grated orange rind
½ teaspoon cinnamon
¼ teaspoon lemon extract

1 quart butter pecan or vanilla
   ice cream, softened
9-inch graham-cracker crust
   (page 139)
⅓ cup finely chopped pecans or
   walnuts
1 tablespoon granulated sugar

In saucepan combine first 5 ingredients. Heat gently, stirring until sugar is dissolved. Add lemon extract and set aside to cool. Then fold carefully into softened ice cream until marbleized. Turn into pie shell. Mix nuts and granulated sugar and sprinkle on pie. Freeze all day or overnight. Let stand at room temperature a few minutes before cutting and serving. Serves 6 to 8.

BLUEBERRY ICE CREAM MOLD

1 pint blueberries
½ cup sugar
1 envelope unflavored gelatin
Dash of salt

1 tablespoon lemon juice
1 egg white
Vanilla ice cream (about 1 quart)

Cook blueberries with ¾ cup water and the sugar about 5 minutes. Strain (you will need 1⅔ cups). Dissolve gelatin in ¼ cup cold water, add to hot mixture and stir until dissolved. Add salt and lemon juice. Pour into pan and freeze. Beat with electric mixer until light. Add stiffly beaten egg white and beat gently to combine. Put in 6-cup mold and freeze. When frozen enough to hold its shape, make a hole in center and push mixture up sides to line mold. Fill with softened ice cream and freeze. Unmold by dipping quickly into warm water. Put back in freezer until serving time. Serves 8.

ICE CREAM CRUNCH

Deceptively delicious!

2 tablespoons butter or
   margarine
1 cup ready-to-eat cereal
   (cornflakes, wheat flakes or
   rice puffs), slightly crushed

½ cup chopped walnuts
¼ cup packed brown sugar
1 quart ice cream (any flavor),
   softened

Mix all ingredients except ice cream in large baking pan. Toast in preheated 350°F. oven 12 minutes or until golden brown, stirring twice. Spread half the mixture in 8 x 8 x 2-inch baking pan, then spread with ice cream. Sprinkle with remaining mixture. Cover and freeze until firm. Cut in squares. Serves 8.

FROZEN RASPBERRY TART

This is a superb alternative to the usual, albeit delicious, room-temperature tart.

Almond Pastry (page 140)
1 package (10 ounces) frozen
   raspberries, thawed
1 cup sugar
2 egg whites
1 tablespoon lemon juice

⅛ teaspoon salt
1½ cups heavy cream
½ teaspoon almond extract
Chopped pistachios or other nuts
   or sliced almonds

Prepare and bake pastry; cool. Set a few raspberries aside for decoration and put remainder with their syrup and next 4 ingredients in large bowl of electric mixer. Beat until stiff. Whip 1 cup cream and fold with almond flavoring into first mixture. Pour onto crust in pan and freeze until firm. When ready to serve, place on serving platter. Remove rim of pan and decorate tart with remaining cream, whipped, nuts and reserved raspberries. Serve in wedges. Serves 8 to 10.

17
PASTRY AND CRUSTS

Many a cook's reputation is made by the pie he or she can bake and, indisputably, a light-textured, flaky crust is the all-important element of success. A tender crust depends on accurate measuring—too much flour makes it tough; too much shortening makes it soggy. As with cakes, pie dough requires a light, quick hand; just enough to blend flour and shortening, and the minimum handling in rolling out the dough. The experienced pastry maker knows the secrets of making a perfect crust—gathering dough into a ball, covering it with plastic wrap and chilling it thoroughly in the refrigerator (4–6 hours or overnight) before working with it. This assures a pliable, easy-to-work piece of pastry that barely needs handling at all.

To roll dough, use as little flour as possible—just enough to keep the work surface and rolling pin from sticking. Divide the dough in half for a two-crust pie and roll out the bottom crust first. Roll out from the center in firm, even strokes, lifting the roller after each pass over the dough, to avoid too much handling. Roll the bottom crust out at least two inches larger than the pie pan, and an eighth of an inch thick. Use the same method to roll out the top crust, which should just fit the top of the pie pan.

Whether filled or prebaked empty, most crusts are put into a hot (400°F. or above) oven for part, if not all, of the cooking time. This assures a light, airy texture, as the cool dough expands rapidly in a hot oven. Roll dough up onto a rolling pin or fold it into quarters with your hands to transfer it to the pan. Press out any air bubbles. The pie shell is now ready for filling or baking empty.

Many of the recipes in this book call for a baked pie shell. Before baking an empty pie shell, prick the bottom surface, at random, with a fork and bake at 425°F.–450°F. for about twelve minutes, checking every five minutes to press out air bubbles that may have formed. The standard method for eliminating air bubbles in tart pastry is to put a sheet of lightweight aluminum foil into the pan over the crust, fill it with dried beans to weight down the crust and bake the crust as directed above. Cool before filling.

A filled, one- or two-crust pie in a crust that has not been prebaked is usually put into the oven at 425°F. for 10 or 15 minutes and then at 350°F. until the pie is cooked to the time specified in each recipe.

Decorative edges, pressed with a fork or fluted by hand, are not only attractive but also, with fruit and berry pies, help to keep juices from running over. Cheesecake crusts are included at the end of this chapter. These are usually pressed by hand into the bottom of a springform pan and baked as specified in individual recipes.

Basic Crusts and Tart Shells

PASTRY

*A basic dough that makes enough pastry for one
2-crust 9-inch pie or two 9-inch pie shells.*

2 cups all-purpose flour	⅔ cup vegetable shortening
1 teaspoon salt	4 tablespoons (about) ice water

Mix well flour and salt. Cut in shortening with 2 knives or pastry blender until mixture resembles coarse meal. Sprinkle the ice water lightly over mixture and work in gently with fork (add only enough water to hold particles together). Gather dough into ball and divide in half. Chill thoroughly before rolling out.

For Pie Shells:
Roll each half on lightly floured board to form a circle about 12 inches in diameter. Ease into 9-inch pie pan. Trim edges, leaving about ½-inch overhang. Crimp edges. Prebake at 425°F. for 12–15 minutes or, for future use, freeze at this stage uncooked until hard, then stack shells together, wrap well and put back in freezer.

RICH TART PASTRY SHELL

*This crust will fill a 9-inch loose-bottom pan. Double
the recipe for two-crust latticed tart, or for 6 medium
tart shells.*

1 cup all-purpose flour	1 egg yolk
1 tablespoon sugar	1 tablespoon ice water
6 tablespoons butter or	
margarine, at room	
temperature but not soft	

Mix flour and sugar in bowl, then work in butter with fingertips. Add egg yolk and water and work with fingers until dough holds together (don't overwork). Pat in flat round, wrap and chill until firm enough to roll. Roll on lightly floured board or between 2 sheets waxed paper to fit 9-inch loose-bottom tart pan. Remove top paper and flop pastry over pan, centering. Let pastry slip down into pan, then gently pull off paper. Use fingers to press pastry into pan; even off rim and chill shell. Bake in preheated 375°F. oven, pricking shell with fork whenever bubbles form, 15 minutes or until lightly browned.

TO MAKE SMALL TART SHELLS

Cut chilled pastry (above) in 4 to 6 (10 to 12 if doubling the recipe) equal pieces. Roll each piece on lightly floured surface to a diameter of 5 inches. Fit in scalloped tart pans, pressing pastry well into scallops. Even off edges with thumb. Then prick bottoms with fork, set pans on cookie sheet and bake in moderate oven (375°F.) 10 to 12 minutes or until golden brown. Cool slightly, then carefully turn out into hand and put on cake rack to cool completely. **NOTE:** If desired, 1 teaspoon grated lemon rind can be added to pastry with egg yolks. Other tart pans can be used. Roll pastry to ⅛-inch thickness and cut in rounds 1 inch larger than diameter of pans.

SWEET-CRISP PIE SHELL

This is a slight variation of the Rich Tart Pastry shell.

1 cup all-purpose flour	1 egg yolk
1 tablespoon sugar	1 tablespoon ice water
6 tablespoons butter or margarine	

Combine in mixing bowl flour and sugar. Cut in butter or margarine until particles are very fine. Beat egg yolk with ice water. Pour over dry mixture and stir with fork to dampen. Then work with hands until dough is smooth and holds together. Roll dough on lightly floured board to 9-inch circle. Transfer to 9-inch pie pan and press firmly over bottom and up sides, stretching to build up edges. Flute edges and prick bottom. Chill 30 minutes. Bake in preheated 350°F. oven with rack in low position 10 minutes.

BASIC FRUIT-TART CRUST

Proportioned to fill a 7½-inch loose-bottom tart pan.

¾ cup all-purpose flour
1 tablespoon sugar
⅛ teaspoon salt

3 tablespoons butter
1 tablespoon shortening

Mix the dry ingredients together, then cut in butter and shortening in small pieces and toss (resulting pieces should be about the size of cornflakes). Sprinkle with 2 tablespoons cold water and form into ball with hands. Then, on floured board, roll out twice to blend in shortening. Form into ball, wrap in waxed paper and refrigerate 2 hours (or about 1 hour in freezer). Preheat oven to 400°F. When dough is chilled, roll out 2 inches larger than tart pan. Roll dough onto rolling pin, place tart pan on board and reverse dough onto pan. Tuck in corners and edges evenly. Trim any excess from edges and save dough in case repairs are needed later. Now prick bottom of dough with tines of fork (prick every inch). Butter one side of sheet of foil and tuck into pan to conform to shape of crust. Fill foil with dried beans. Bake 10 minutes. Take from oven and remove foil with beans. Prick bottom of crust again with fork. Put back in oven another 10 minutes or until crust turns a light golden color. When crust is done, remove from oven and set aside to cool.

BUTTER PASTRY

1½ cups flour
¾ teaspoon salt

½ cup plus 1 tablespoon butter
    or margarine, slightly softened
3 tablespoons ice water

Stir together flour and salt. Cut in butter or margarine until particles are size of small peas. Sprinkle with ice water; toss with fork to mix. Gather into ball; wrap in waxed paper or plastic wrap. **NOTE:** Use for any latticed fruit pie.

TWO-CRUST LEMON PASTRY

1½ cups flour
2 tablespoons sugar
¾ teaspoon salt
¾ teaspoon grated lemon peel

½ cup shortening
1½ tablespoons lemon juice
1 tablespoon water

In large bowl combine flour, sugar, salt and peel. With pastry blender cut in shortening until mixture resembles coarse crumbs. With fork, stir in lemon juice and water. Press into ball. Roll out two thirds of pastry and line 9-inch pie plate. Roll out remaining one third of pastry to place over pie filling. Bake pie as directed or, for fruit pies, at 400°F. for 20 minutes and 350°F. for next 15 minutes or until crust is golden brown.

SPECIAL FLAN RING PASTRY SHELL

This is the pastry used in the Peach-Pear Flan (page 82), a Silver Spoon Award winner. Though similar to the recipe above, it is reprinted here exactly as is.

1 cup flour
Dash of salt
½ cup butter or margarine,
  softened, cut in small pieces

1 egg yolk
1 tablespoon sugar
Ice water

In large bowl mix flour and salt; make a well in center. Place butter, yolk and sugar in well; with fingers mix until blended. Gradually work in flour, adding water if necessary, until dough is smooth and holds together. Shape in ball, wrap tight and chill at least 1 hour or until firm enough to roll. On well-floured surface roll pastry into 11-inch circle. Carefully place in 9-inch quiche pan, flan ring or pie plate. (Pastry is very tender and may break. Press together to patch.) Trim edges as desired. Prick bottom at 1-inch intervals. Bake in preheated 375°F. oven 20 minutes or until lightly browned. Cool in pan on rack.

ALMOND TARTS

Bake ahead and freeze; serve unfilled or, for a quick dessert, fill with whipped cream and berries or a dab of jam.

½ cup butter or margarine,
  softened
¼ cup sugar
¼ teaspoon almond extract
⅛ teaspoon salt

1 egg white
½ cup blanched almonds, ground
  or grated
1¼ cups flour

In large bowl of mixer cream butter, sugar, almond extract and salt until fluffy. Add egg white and beat well. Stir in almonds and flour until blended. Wrap airtight and chill 1 hour or longer. Pinch off tablespoonfuls of dough and place in assorted fluted cookie molds (about 3½- or 2½-inch size). With lightly floured thumb press dough against bottom and sides, forming shell about ⅛-inch thick. Place molds on cookie sheet and bake in preheated 350°F. oven 10 to 12 minutes or until golden. While still slightly warm, turn molds upside down on cookie sheet and tap gently with spoon to loosen shells. Cool completely on rack. Makes about 24. **NOTE:** Fluted cookie molds are available in utensil specialty shops and in many houseware departments of large stores.

Pie Shell Variations Using Flour

ALMOND CRUST

This is a delicious crust for a baked-shell or deep-dish pie.

1 cup flour
½ teaspoon salt
6 tablespoons butter or margarine

¼ cup almonds, sliced
Scant 2 tablespoons cold water
½ teaspoon almond extract

Stir together flour and salt. Cut in butter or margarine until particles are size of small peas. Stir in sliced almonds. Sprinkle with cold water mixed with almond extract and toss to mix. Gather into ball. Roll out on lightly floured board to fit top of baking dish; cut decorative vents.

CHOCOLATE-WALNUT PIE SHELL

1 cup flour
¼ cup finely chopped walnuts
1 square (1 ounce) unsweetened chocolate, grated coarse

2 tablespoons sugar
⅛ teaspoon salt
⅓ cup shortening
About 2 tablespoons cold water

In bowl mix flour, walnuts, chocolate, sugar and salt. Cut in shortening until mixture resembles coarse crumbs. Sprinkle with water, about 1 tablespoon at a time, mixing just until ball forms. On lightly floured surface roll out pastry to large circle. Fit into 9-inch pie plate; trim and flute edge. Prick bottom and sides with fork. Bake in preheated 375°F. oven 20 to 25 minutes or until lightly browned at edge. Cool. If desired, roll out and bake any scraps of dough in ungreased pan 15 to 20 minutes or until lightly browned. Cool. Crumble coarse and use as garnish.

SESAME-SEED PIE SHELL

1 cup all-purpose flour
½ teaspoon salt

¼ cup toasted sesame seed
⅓ cup solid vegetable shortening

Put first 3 ingredients in bowl and cut in shortening. Mixing with fork, add cold water a little at a time until dry ingredients just hold together. Shape in ball and roll out on lightly floured board to ⅛-inch thickness. Line 9-inch pie pan and flute edges. Prick well with fork and bake in very hot oven (450°F.) 12 minutes or until golden brown; cool.

NUT PIE SHELL

⅓ cup pecans and walnuts, combined
1 cup all-purpose flour

¼ teaspoon salt
½ cup butter or margarine
Scant 3 tablespoons ice water

Chop pecans and walnuts very fine. Combine with flour and salt in mixing bowl. Cut in butter or margarine until particles are the size of peas. Sprinkle with ice water and stir with fork to dampen, then form in ball with hands. Roll out on lightly floured board, fit in 9-inch pie pan and flute edges. Press firmly to bottom of pan, then chill 30 minutes. Bake in preheated 350°F. oven with rack in low position 10 minutes.

WHOLE-WHEAT PIE SHELL

1¼ cups whole-wheat flour
½ teaspoon salt

½ cup solid white vegetable shortening

Put flour and salt in bowl, then cut in shortening with pastry blender or 2 knives. Mixing with fork, add enough cold water to hold mixture together. Pull into ball and roll on floured board to ⅛-inch thickness. Fit in 9-inch pie pan, trim edges and flute. Prick with fork and bake in preheated 450°F. oven about 12 minutes.

Pie Shell Variations Using Cracker or Wafer Crumbs

GRAHAM-CRACKER PIE SHELL

An unbaked version.

1¼ cups graham-cracker crumbs
3 tablespoons sugar

6 tablespoons butter or margarine, melted

Mix all ingredients. Press firmly in 9-inch pie plate. Chill in freezer 15 minutes or in refrigerator 1 hour.

BAKED GRAHAM-CRACKER CRUST

Combine all ingredients listed in recipe above. Press firmly on bottom and sides of 9-inch pie pan and bake in preheated 375°F. oven 6 to 8 minutes or until edges are brown. (Or if preferred, chill pie crust in refrigerator about 45 minutes.)

ALMOND-GRAHAM CRUST

1 cup graham-cracker crumbs
½ cup ground almonds

3 tablespoons sugar
3 tablespoons butter or
   margarine, softened

Mix all ingredients well. Press on bottom and sides of 9-inch pie plate. Bake in preheated 400°F. oven 8 to 10 minutes or until golden brown. Cool completely on rack.

WALNUT CRUMB CRUST

1¼ cups vanilla wafer crumbs
¼ cup walnuts, chopped fine

2 tablespoons sugar
5 tablespoons butter, softened

Combine all ingredients. Press firmly on bottom and sides of 9-inch pie pan. Bake in preheated 375°F. oven 8 minutes.

ORANGE-GINGERSNAP CRUMB CRUST

1¼ cups finely crushed
   gingersnaps
¼ cup butter or margarine,
   softened

1 teaspoon grated orange rind
¼ teaspoon ginger

Combine gingersnaps and butter. Add 1 teaspoon grated orange rind and ¼ teaspoon ginger. Press into 9-inch pie pan and bake in moderate oven (375°F.) 8 minutes.

Cheesecake Crusts

ALMOND PASTRY

¼ cup butter or margarine,
　softened
2 tablespoons sugar
1 egg yolk

¾ cup all-purpose flour, lightly
　spooned into cup
¼ cup minced blanched almonds

Cream first 3 ingredients until light. Stir in flour and almonds until well mixed. Press onto bottom of 9-inch springform pan 3 inches deep. Bake in preheated 400°F. oven 12 minutes or until golden brown.

GRAHAM-NUT CRUST

¾ cup graham-cracker crumbs
¼ cup butter or margarine,
　melted

¼ cup ground almonds
3 tablespoons sugar

Combine graham-cracker crumbs, butter or margarine, almonds and sugar. Press on bottom and 1 inch up sides of 8- or 9-inch springform pan.

VANILLA-WAFER CRUST

1 cup vanilla-wafer crumbs
2 tablespoons sugar
½ teaspoon cinnamon

¼ teaspoon instant coffee
　granules
¼ cup butter or margarine,
　melted

Combine all ingredients. Press on bottom of 9-inch springform or other loose-bottom pan.

SPICY CRUMB CRUST

1 cup vanilla-wafer crumbs
¼ cup butter or margarine,
　melted

2 tablespoons brown sugar
½ teaspoon ground allspice

Combine all ingredients. Pat on bottom and about 1 inch up sides of well-buttered loose-bottom 9 x 3-inch round pan. Bake in moderate oven (350°F.) about 8 minutes.

COOKIE-DOUGH CRUST

1 cup all-purpose flour
¼ cup sugar
½ cup butter or margarine

1 egg yolk
1 teaspoon vanilla

Combine flour and sugar. Cut in butter or margarine until particles are fine. Beat egg yolk with vanilla, then work into flour mixture with fork or fingertips until well blended. Shape in ball, put on small piece of waxed paper and flatten to pancake shape. Chill 10 minutes. Put in bottom of 9-inch springform or other loose-bottom pan and press with fingers to cover bottom and 1 inch up sides. Bake in preheated 400°F. oven 12 to 14 minutes or until lightly browned.

COCONUT CRUST

⅔ cup vanilla-wafer crumbs
⅓ cup flaked coconut

1 teaspoon grated orange rind
2 tablespoons butter or
    margarine, melted

Combine all ingredients. Press on bottom of 9-inch springform or other loose-bottom pan. Chill.

CHOCOLATE-WAFER CRUST

1 cup chocolate-wafer crumbs,
    crushed fine

2 tablespoons sugar
¼ cup melted butter

Combine all ingredients. Press on bottom of 9-inch springform or other loose-bottom pan.

CHOCOLATE-CINNAMON CRUST

1¼ cups chocolate-wafer crumbs
¼ to ½ teaspoon ground
    cinnamon

¼ cup butter or margarine,
    melted

Combine and mix all ingredients. With damp fingers, press onto bottom and sides of 9-inch springform pan or 9-inch loose-bottom layer-cake pan. Chill while mixing cheese-cake filling.

18
FROSTINGS, ICINGS, FILLINGS AND GLAZES

Frostings, Icings and Fillings

Boiled Frosting

1½ cups sugar
½ teaspoon cream of tartar
⅛ teaspoon salt
½ cup hot water
4 egg whites (about ½ cup)

Combine sugar, cream of tartar, salt and water in small saucepan. Cook rapidly *without stirring* to soft-ball stage (240°F. on candy thermometer), 6 to 8 minutes. Beat egg whites in large bowl of mixer until stiff but not dry. Pour hot syrup in thin stream into egg whites, beating constantly at high speed until frosting holds stiff peaks, is shiny and smooth. Will fill and frost three 9-inch layers.

Sea-Foam Frosting

2 egg whites
1½ cups brown sugar, packed
⅛ teaspoon salt
⅓ cup water
1 teaspoon vanilla

Put egg whites, brown sugar, salt and water in top part of double boiler. Beat 1 minute with rotary or electric beater to mix thoroughly. Then put over boiling water and beat 7 minutes or until frosting stands in peaks. Remove from water and add vanilla. Beat 1 minute longer. Will fill and frost two 9-inch layers.

Meringue Frosting

4 egg whites
⅛ teaspoon salt
½ cup sugar

In large bowl of electric mixer beat egg whites and salt at medium speed until soft peaks form. Increase speed to high and gradually beat in sugar, beating until stiff peaks form. Will frost one filled 2-layer 9-inch torte or layer cake.

Butter Cream Frosting

¾ cup butter, softened
2 egg yolks
1 teaspoon vanilla
2¼ cups confectioners' sugar

Beat together thoroughly butter, egg yolks and vanilla. Gradually add confectioners' sugar, beating until smooth. Will fill and frost two 9-inch layers.

Mocha Butter Cream

⅓ cup water
3 tablespoons instant coffee
3 squares (1 ounce each) unsweetened
  chocolate
1½ cups butter or margarine, softened
2½ cups confectioners' sugar
3 egg yolks
1 teaspoon vanilla

In small heavy saucepan over very low heat stir gently water, coffee and chocolate until melted and smooth. Cool. In small bowl of mixer cream butter, sugar and yolks until smooth and well blended. Gradually add chocolate mixture; beat just until well blended. Stir in vanilla. Will fill and frost three 8-inch layers.

Chocolate Frosting I

1¼ cups sugar
½ cup water
2 egg whites
3 tablespoons grated unsweetened chocolate
½ teaspoon vanilla

Cook sugar and water until mixture spins a thread (236°F. on candy thermometer). Beat egg whites until stiff. Gradually add syrup, beating. Beat in chocolate and vanilla. Will frost one 10-inch tube cake.

Chocolate Frosting II

½ cup butter or margarine, softened
2 squares unsweetened chocolate, melted
2 teaspoons vanilla
2 cups confectioners' sugar
2 tablespoons milk

Cream butter or margarine until light and fluffy; blend in chocolate and vanilla; gradually beat in confectioners' sugar alternately with milk until smooth.

Chocolate Frosting III

1 square unsweetened chocolate
2 tablespoons butter
Dash of salt
1 cup confectioners' sugar
Hot water
1 egg yolk
¼ teaspoon vanilla

Melt chocolate and butter together. Beat in salt, confectioners' sugar and enough hot water to make of spreading consistency. Beat in egg yolk and vanilla. Will frost 12 cupcakes.

Rich Chocolate Frosting

6 tablespoons butter, softened
6 squares unsweetened chocolate, melted
3⅓ cups confectioners' sugar, sifted
⅓ cup water
6 egg yolks
1½ teaspoons vanilla

Cream butter in large mixing bowl. Add chocolate, sugar and water. Mix well. Add egg yolks, one at a time, beating well after each addition. Add vanilla and beat until smooth. Chill 10 minutes before frosting cake. Will frost one 10-inch tube cake.

Dark-Chocolate Butter Frosting

½ cup butter or margarine, softened
6 squares (6 ounces) unsweetened chocolate,
  melted and cooled
3 egg yolks
⅓ cup hot water
2½ cups unsifted confectioners' sugar
1 teaspoon vanilla

In large bowl of mixer beat butter, chocolate and egg yolks until well blended. Beat in water. Gradually beat in sugar until smooth and glossy. Beat in vanilla. Will generously fill and frost two 9-inch cake layers.

Velvety Chocolate Frosting

¼ cup hot water
2¼ cups confectioners' sugar
4 squares (1 ounce each) unsweetened
   chocolate, melted
4 egg yolks
¼ cup butter or margarine, melted
1 teaspoon vanilla

Add hot water and sugar to chocolate and mix well. Add egg yolks, one at a time, beating well after each. Slowly add butter, then vanilla, and beat until smooth. If too thin to spread immediately, let stand a few minutes to thicken. Will frost a 13 x 9-inch rectangle or two 8-inch cake layers.

Chocolate Icing

5 ounces semisweet chocolate
½ cup heavy cream

In heavy saucepan, over low heat melt chocolate with heavy cream, stirring until smooth. Will frost a 1-layer cake or torte.

Lemon Confectioners' Sugar Frosting

⅓ cup butter or margarine, softened
1½ cups confectioners' sugar
1 to 2 tablespoons lemon juice

With fork mix butter and sugar until thoroughly blended. Add lemon juice; beat until smooth and of spreading consistency. Makes about 1½ cups.

Orange Icing

2 tablespoons butter or margarine, softened
3 cups confectioners' sugar
¼ cup orange juice
2 teaspoons lemon juice

In small bowl beat together all ingredients until well blended. Makes about 1–1½ cups.

Orange Frosting

½ cup butter or margarine
1 cup confectioners' sugar
2 teaspoons grated orange rind
1 tablespoon orange juice

Cream butter or margarine and sugar until light. Add grated orange rind and about 1 tablespoon orange juice. Will frost two 8-inch sponge layers.

Creamy Lemon Frosting

¼ cup butter or margarine
⅛ teaspoon salt
2 cups confectioners' sugar
1 egg yolk
½ teaspoon grated lemon rind
1 tablespoon (about) milk

Cream butter until soft. Add salt, then part of sugar gradually, blending after each addition. Add egg yolk and rind and mix well. Add remaining sugar alternately with milk until of right consistency to spread, beating after each addition until smooth. Makes 1¼ cups.

Tropical Butter Frosting

¼ cup butter or margarine
1 box (1 pound) confectioners' sugar
¼ cup lightly drained crushed pineapple
2 tablespoons sour cream
¾ cup flaked coconut
2 teaspoons coarsely grated orange peel
1 teaspoon vanilla
¼ teaspoon salt

In large bowl of mixer beat butter until soft. Gradually beat in sugar alternately with pineapple and sour cream until mixture is fluffy and smoothly blended. Stir in coconut, orange peel, vanilla and salt. Will frost three 9-inch layers.

Coconut Frosting

1½ cups confectioners' sugar
2 tablespoons lemon juice
3 tablespoons coconut

Stir sugar and lemon juice together until smooth. Spread on top of cake and sprinkle with coconut. Will frost two 9 x 5 x 3-inch loaf cakes or one 8-inch square cake.

Lane Frosting

1½ cups seedless raisins
½ cup rye or bourbon
1½ cups quartered candied cherries
12 egg yolks
1¾ cups sugar
½ teaspoon salt
¾ cup butter or margarine, softened
1½ cups coarsely chopped pecans
1½ cups shredded fresh coconut

Put first 3 ingredients in container with tightly fitting lid and let stand at least 2 hours, preferably overnight. Combine next 4 ingredients in top part of double boiler, put over simmering water and cook, stirring, until sugar is dissolved and mixture is slightly thickened and almost translucent. Remove from heat and add fruit mixture with the whiskey, nuts and coconut. Mix well and cool. A quantity recipe that will frost 45 cupcakes.

Cranberry and Cream-Cheese Frosting

1 package (3 ounces) cream cheese
¼ cup whole-cranberry sauce
2 cups confectioners' sugar

Soften cream cheese in small bowl of electric mixer. Beat in cranberry sauce. Add 2 cups confectioners' sugar, beating until smooth and of spreading consistency. Will frost one 13 x 9 x 2-inch loaf cake.

Quick Caramel Frosting

¼ cup butter or margarine
¾ cup brown sugar, packed down
3 tablespoons milk
2 cups confectioners' sugar
1 teaspoon vanilla

Melt shortening in saucepan. Stir in brown sugar and cook, stirring, 2 minutes. Slowly add milk and bring to boil. Remove from heat and stir in sugar and vanilla. Will frost one 13 x 9 x 2-inch loaf cake.

Dried Fruits Frosting

1 cup sugar
½ teaspoon cream of tartar
⅛ teaspoon salt
⅓ cup hot water
3 egg whites (about ½ cup)
5 figs, cut in small pieces
⅔ cup each, raisins and chopped nuts

Combine sugar, cream of tartar, salt and water in small saucepan. Cook rapidly *without stirring* to soft-ball stage (240°F. on candy thermometer). Meanwhile beat egg whites in large bowl of electric mixer until stiff but not dry Pour hot syrup in fine stream into egg whites, beating constantly at high speed until frosting holds stiff peaks and is shiny and smooth. Cool. Stir in figs, raisins and nuts. Will fill and frost two 8-inch layers.

Cream-Cheese Frosting I

1 package (3 ounces) cream cheese, at room temperature
3 tablespoons butter or margarine, softened
Pinch of salt
½ teaspoon vanilla
1½ cups confectioners' sugar

Mix all ingredients together until smooth. Will frost one 13 x 9 x 2-inch loaf cake.

Cream-Cheese Frosting II

2 packages (3 ounces each) cream cheese
1 box (1 pound) confectioners' sugar
About 2 tablespoons orange or lemon juice
1 teaspoon vanilla
1 teaspoon grated orange or lemon peel, or to
    taste

In small bowl of mixer beat cheese until light. Gradually beat in sugar. Thin frosting, as you beat, with juice until it is of good spreading consistency. Add vanilla and grated peel. Will frost two 9-inch layers.

Almond-Paste Frosting

This is a traditional element in many torte recipes. The frosting rolls out in one sheet to cover the top of a 9-inch round cake.

1 cup blanched almonds
Confectioners' sugar
1 egg white
1 teaspoon almond extract

Grate almonds in blender until *very fine* (or put through nut grinder twice). In mixing bowl combine almonds with 1½ cups confectioners' sugar, the egg white, and extract. Blend with fork, then knead well with hands until paste is very smooth and sugar has been absorbed completely. Add more sugar if paste is still sticky. Gather into ball, wrap in plastic and chill until ready to use. Place on pastry cloth sprinkled with confectioners' sugar. With rolling pin covered with stockinette roll out 12-inch circle, trim with pastry wheel and place over stacked, chilled torte. (To lift circle without tearing, fold loosely in quarters or roll over rolling pin.)

Vanilla Frosting

2 tablespoons butter
Dash of salt
2¼ cups confectioners' sugar
3 tablespoons milk
½ teaspoon vanilla

Mix all ingredients until well combined. Makes enough to frost one 13 x 9 x 2-inch or one 9-inch single layer cake.

Creamy Molasses Frosting

⅓ cup butter or margarine, softened
3 cups confectioners' sugar
1 egg white
1 teaspoon vanilla
1 tablespoon molasses
1 to 1½ tablespoons milk

Cream shortening until fluffy. Add 1 cup confectioners' sugar, egg white and vanilla and mix well. Gradually beat in 2 cups confectioners' sugar alternately with molasses and milk. Blend well until smooth and of spreading consistency. Will frost one 13 x 9 x 2-inch loaf cake.

Coffee Frosting

Make a day or two before using.

3 cups sugar
⅔ cup light corn syrup
1 cup light cream
2 tablespoons butter or margarine
2 teaspoons instant-coffee powder
½ teaspoon cinnamon

Put first 3 ingredients in deep saucepan, bring to boil and boil, without stirring, to a temperature of 236°F. on candy thermometer, or until small amount of mixture forms a soft ball when dropped in very cold water. Remove from heat and cool to lukewarm (110°F.). Add remaining ingredients and beat at medium speed of electric mixer 5 minutes, or until creamy. (Frosting will have consistency of thick syrup and will not be crystalline.) Store, covered, in refrigerator at least 6 hours. When ready to use, put needed amount in top part of double boiler over boiling water and stir 1 to 2 minutes, or until of spreading consistency. Makes enough frosting to cover tops of four 9" layers.

Custard Filling

For any basic fruit tart.

½ cup sugar
3 egg yolks
6 tablespoons flour
1 cup milk
2 teaspoons vanilla
1 tablespoon butter

With spoon, beat sugar and egg yolks together 5 minutes or until smooth, then beat in flour. Bring milk almost to boil in small heavy saucepan. Just before boiling point is reached, remove from heat. Start beating egg-yolk mixture again and slowly pour hot milk into it. Put mixture back in saucepan and beat with spoon or wire whisk over low heat until thickened. Continue beating and cooking 2 more minutes, then remove from heat. Stir in vanilla and butter, then set aside to cool.

Custard-Cream Filling

¼ cup sugar
1 tablespoon cornstarch
2 teaspoons unflavored gelatin
1 cup milk, scalded
2 egg yolks
2 teaspoons vanilla
1 tablespoon orange-flavored
　　liqueur (optional)
1 cup heavy cream, softly whipped

In small saucepan combine sugar, cornstarch and gelatin. Gradually pour in milk, beating with whisk. Beat in egg yolks and cook over low heat, beating constantly, until mixture coats spoon and is smooth (about 3 minutes). Stir in vanilla and liqueur. Cool until slightly thickened, stirring occasionally. Fold in whipped cream; chill until of spreading consistency. Will fill and frost two 9-inch layers.

Bourbon Filling

8 egg yolks
1 cup each, sugar and raisins
1 cup fresh or canned shredded coconut
½ cup butter or margarine, softened
¼ cup bourbon or blended whiskey

Combine egg yolks, sugar, raisins, coconut and butter in top of double boiler. Cook and stir over simmering water until thick and mixture mounds when dropped from spoon, 15 to 20 minutes. Remove from heat and stir in bourbon. Cool. Will generously fill three 9-inch layers.

Chocolate-Orange Filling

5 squares (5 ounces) semisweet chocolate
⅔ cup butter or margarine, softened but not
　　runny
2 cups confectioners' sugar
1 egg yolk
¼ cup finely chopped candied orange peel

Melt chocolate in double boiler over hot water and cool. In small bowl of mixer, cream butter until light and fluffy. Continue beating and add confectioners' sugar gradually. Blend in cooled chocolate with egg yolk. Stir in candied orange peel. Will fill one sponge roll.

French Chocolate Cake-Roll Filling

8 squares (8 ounces) semisweet chocolate
¼ cup hot coffee or water (or two tablespoons each)
½ teaspoon vanilla

Melt chocolate in top of double boiler over hot water. Stir in coffee or water and vanilla. Cool a few minutes until slightly thickened. Spread over warm cake and roll as directed. Cool at room temperature until chocolate hardens, about 4 hours. Will fill one sponge roll.

Apricot Filling

1 cup dried apricots
1 cup water
⅔ cup granulated sugar
1½ teaspoons vanilla

Place apricots and water in saucepan; bring to boil. Cover, then simmer 10 minutes or until liquid is absorbed. Mash thoroughly. Stir in sugar and vanilla. Cook and stir until thickened. Will fill one sponge roll.

Raisin-Cream Filling

¾ cup raisins, frozen
1½ cups ground walnuts
1½ cups dairy sour cream
1 cup confectioners' sugar
¾ teaspoon vanilla.

Chop raisins, half at a time, in blender. In blender or bowl mix walnuts, sour cream, sugar and vanilla with raisins. Blend until smooth. Will fill one sponge roll.

Lemon Cream I

¾ cup heavy cream
1 tablespoon sugar
¾ teaspoon lemon juice

Beat all ingredients until stiff. Makes 1½ cups; will frost one 9-inch square loaf cake.

Lemon Cream II

4 egg yolks
½ cup sugar
Grated peel of 2 lemons
½ cup fresh lemon juice
¼ cup butter or margarine, softened

In top of double boiler combine egg yolks, sugar, lemon peel and juice. Cook and beat over simmering water until cream thickens and is smooth and lemon-colored (about 5 minutes). Beat in butter or margarine. Cool, stirring occasionally, then cover loosely and chill. Stir before using. Will fill two 8- or 9-inch layers.

10 Whipped-Cream Filling Variations:

Heavy cream doubles in volume when whipped.

Sweetened Whipped Cream

1 cup heavy cream
¼ cup sugar
½ teaspoon vanilla

Whip cream until it holds soft peaks. Add sugar and vanilla and continue to whip until sugar is blended. Be careful not to overbeat. Use as filling in cream puffs, frosting on angel-food cake or filling for one sponge roll. Makes about 2 cups.

Amber Whipped Cream

½ cup heavy cream
2 tablespoons light-brown sugar

Put cream and sugar in bowl and chill 1 hour, then whip until stiff. Serve on fruit or use as a topping for cakes. Makes 1 cup.

Coffee-Flavored Whipped Cream

2 cups heavy cream
3 tablespoons sugar
2 teaspoons instant coffee

Beat cream until soft peaks form. Gradually beat in sugar, beating until stiff. Fold in coffee powder. Will fill and frost two 9-inch cake or torte layers.

Chocolate Whipped Cream

6 ounces (1½ bars) sweet cooking chocolate
1 teaspoon vanilla
1½ cups heavy cream, whipped

Put chocolate and 4½ tablespoons water in heavy saucepan and put over low heat. Stir until melted and smooth. Cool; add vanilla. Fold into whipped cream. Will fill and frost two 9-inch layers or three 8-inch layers.

Brandy Whipped Cream I

1½ cups heavy cream
2 tablespoons sugar
1 to 2 tablespoons brandy

Beat cream until soft peaks form. Gradually beat in sugar, beating until stiff. Fold in brandy. Makes about 2½ cups; will frost two 8- or 9-inch cake or torte layers.

Brandy Whipped Cream II

½ cup heavy cream
2 tablespoons sugar
1 tablespoon brandy

Stir all ingredients together in large mixing bowl. Chill at least 1 hour. Whip until soft peaks form. Will generously frost one 9-inch pie or one 9-inch layer.

Rum Whipped Cream

1 cup heavy cream
2 tablespoons sugar
1 to 2 teaspoons dark rum

In small bowl of mixer stir all ingredients together. Chill at least 1 hour. Whip until stiff. Will frost one 9-inch pie or two 9-inch layers.

Cocoa Whipped-Cream Frosting

4 tablespoons sugar
3 tablespoons cocoa
1½ cups heavy cream
½ teaspoon almond extract

In small bowl of mixer mix well sugar with cocoa. Stir in heavy cream and almond extract. Chill with beaters at least 30 minutes. Whip until soft peaks form. Will fill and frost three 8-inch layers.

Mocha Whipped Cream I

½ cup heavy cream
1 teaspoon instant coffee
1 tablespoon confectioners' sugar
¼ teaspoon vanilla

In small chilled bowl of mixer whip with chilled beaters all ingredients until soft peaks form. Will garnish a 9-inch pie, 4 servings chocolate mousse or any other dessert. Double recipe for 2-layer cake frosting or filling.

Mocha Whipped Cream II

½ cup sugar
¼ cup cocoa
1 tablespoon instant coffee
¼ teaspoon salt
2 teaspoons vanilla
1½ cups heavy cream

Place all ingredients in blender. Cover and whip until thick (do not overblend). Use rubber spatula to keep all ingredients flowing to blades. Makes about 2½ cups; will frost two 8-inch cake or torte layers.

Praline Butter Cream

¼ cup unblanched almonds
1 cup sugar
⅓ cup water
4 egg yolks, well beaten
1 cup butter or margarine, softened

Cook and stir almonds and ¼ cup sugar in small heavy skillet over medium heat until sugar is melted and golden brown and almonds are lightly toasted. Pour praline mixture on greased cookie sheet to cool. When hard, break in small pieces, then grate in blender; set aside. Combine remaining ¾ cup sugar and the water in small saucepan and bring to boil over medium heat (do not stir). Cook just until a thin syrup forms and a drop placed between thumb and index finger feels sticky (be careful not to burn fingers), or until candy thermometer reads 220°F. (about 6 minutes). Pour hot syrup in thin stream over yolks, beating constantly. Cool, beating occasionally. Cream butter, then gradually beat in egg-sugar mixture until smooth and thick. Fold in praline. Will fill and frost two 9-inch square or round cake or torte layers.

Lemon Filling

⅔ cup butter or margarine, softened
   but not runny
2 cups confectioners' sugar
1 teaspoon grated lemon rind
2 tablespoons lemon juice

In small bowl of mixer cream butter until light and fluffy. Alternately add sugar with combined lemon rind and juice, beating until smooth. Will fill one sponge roll.

Prune Filling

1 pound dried prunes
1 cup water
½ cup sugar

Put prunes in saucepan with water. Bring to boil, cover and simmer 15 minutes or until soft. Add sugar and simmer 5 minutes longer. Drain prunes; pit and chop or cut fine. Will fill about 2 dozen small tarts (page 82) or one sponge roll.

Orange Filling

2 tablespoons butter or margarine
⅔ cup sugar mixed with 5 tablespoons
   cornstarch
1 cup water
1 can (6 ounces) frozen orange-juice
   concentrate, thawed
Grated peel of ½ lemon
1 tablespoon lemon juice
2 egg yolks, slightly beaten

Melt butter in top of double boiler, then blend in sugar-cornstarch mixture. Stir in water, juice concentrate, lemon peel and juice until well blended. Cook and stir over boiling water until thickened. Cover and cook 5 minutes longer. Slowly stir in egg yolks and mix well. Chill. Will fill three 8-inch layers.

Raspberry Filling and Frosting

1 box (10 ounces) frozen raspberries,
   barely thawed and well drained
1 egg white
1 cup sugar

Put berries in small bowl of electric mixer and add egg white and sugar. Beat until mixture forms peaks. Will fill and frost three 9-inch layers.

Jelly or Jam Cake-Roll Filling

¾ to 1 cup jelly, jam or preserves
1 tablespoon hot water

Blend ingredients and spread over cooled cake. Roll as directed. Will fill one sponge roll.

Glazes

Chocolate Glaze I

2 tablespoons milk
1 tablespoon butter or margarine
1 square (1 ounce) unsweetened chocolate
1 teaspoon vanilla
¾ cup confectioners' sugar

In small saucepan heat milk and shortening over low heat until hot. Add chocolate and stir until melted. Stir in vanilla and sugar. Blend until smooth. Spread while warm. Will glaze top of square or small loaf cake.

Thin Chocolate Glaze

5 squares (5 ounces) semisweet chocolate
⅓ cup hot water

Melt chocolate in a small saucepan or in a double boiler. Stir in hot water until smooth. Spread thin over sponge roll or small loaf cake.

Chocolate Glaze II

2 tablespoons cocoa
1 tablespoon each, oil and corn syrup
2 tablespoons plus 1 teaspoon water
½ teaspoon cinnamon
1 cup confectioners' sugar

In small saucepan combine cocoa, oil, corn syrup, water and cinnamon. Stir over low heat until smooth. Gradually beat in sugar until smooth and shiny. Will glaze an 8- or 9-inch square cake.

Glossy Chocolate Glaze

2 squares (2 ounces) semisweet chocolate *or*
   ⅓ cup semisweet chocolate pieces
2 tablespoons light corn syrup
1 teaspoon brewed coffee

Melt chocolate in top of double boiler over hot water. Stir in corn syrup and coffee. Keep over water until ready to use. Makes about ¼ cup; will glaze one sponge roll. **NOTE:** Recipe can be doubled

Lemon Glaze

1 cup confectioners' sugar
½ teaspoon grated lemon peel
Dash of salt
3 to 4 teaspoons lemon juice

Combine first three ingredients. Beat in enough lemon juice to make a thin glaze. Will glaze one small loaf cake.

Orange Glaze I

1 cup confectioners' sugar
¼ cup orange juice
¼ teaspoon grated orange rind

Mix sugar, juice and rind in a small bowl. Let stand on top of oven or other warm place while cake is baking, stirring once or twice. Will glaze one 9 x 5 x 3-inch loaf.

Orange Glaze II

1 cup confectioners' sugar
1 to 2 tablespoons orange juice

Mix ingredients together until smooth and of spreading consistency. Will glaze one small loaf cake.

Orange Glaze III

2 teaspoons unflavored gelatin
2 tablespoons sugar
¼ cup water
¾ cup orange juice

Combine gelatin, sugar and water in saucepan. Cook over low heat until gelatin is dissolved. Stir in orange juice. Cool until glaze has consistency of unbeaten egg whites. Will glaze one 9-inch cake or torte.

Pineapple Glaze

3 tablespoons sugar
1 tablespoon cornstarch
1 cup unsweetened pineapple juice
¼ teaspoon grated lemon rind

Mix sugar and cornstarch in small saucepan. Stir in pineapple juice and lemon rind. Bring to a boil and cook, stirring, 1 minute or until clear and slightly thickened; cool. Will glaze one pie or cheesecake.

Rum Glaze

1¼ cups confectioners' sugar
1 tablespoon light rum
1 tablespoon water

Mix all ingredients together until smooth. Will glaze one 9- or 10-inch tube or bundt cake.

Rhubarb Glaze

2 cups diced rhubarb, frozen or fresh
¾ cup water
1 envelope unflavored gelatin
¼ cup sugar
Red food coloring, if desired

Combine rhubarb and ½ cup water in saucepan. Slowly bring to boil, cover and simmer 6 to 8 minutes. Strain through fine sieve or cheesecloth. Measure ¾ cup liquid and add food coloring to tint desired shade. Soften gelatin in remaining ¼ cup water in a mixing bowl. Combine rhubarb liquid and sugar in saucepan. Bring to boil and pour over gelatin, stirring until dissolved. Cool until slightly thickened. An excellent glaze for one cheesecake or cheese pie.

19
SAUCES, SYRUPS, TOPPINGS AND GARNISHES

Rich Hot-Fudge Sauce

⅓ cup butter or margarine
2 squares (1 ounce each) unsweetened
    chocolate
2 squares (1 ounce each) semisweet
    chocolate
1 cup sugar
1 cup heavy cream
⅛ teaspoon salt
2 teaspoons vanilla

In large heavy saucepan melt butter and the chocolates over very low heat. Blend in sugar, cream and salt. Stir over low heat until hot and sugar is dissolved, about 5 minutes. Remove from heat; stir in vanilla. Serve warm. Makes about 2⅓ cups. **NOTE:** Store any leftover sauce, covered, in refrigerator. To serve, stir over very low heat until hot, adding a little hot water if too thick or grainy.

Broiled Topping

¾ cup coconut, flaked
½ cup brown sugar, packed
½ cup chopped nuts
¼ cup butter or margarine, melted
3 tablespoons milk or cream

Combine all ingredients and spread over top of a 9-inch square cake. Place under broiler until top is lightly browned.

Bittersweet Chocolate-Rum Sauce

1 cup each, cocoa and sugar
¼ teaspoon salt
¾ cup hot water
2 tablespoons butter or margarine
3 tablespoons dark rum
2 teaspoons vanilla

In small heavy saucepan stir together cocoa, sugar and salt. With whisk gradually beat in water until smooth. Add butter; stir over medium-low heat about 10 minutes or until slightly thickened. Remove from heat; stir in rum and vanilla. Cool, then pour into 1-pint glass jar; cover and store in cool place. Serve warm or cold over ice cream, plain cake or fruits. Makes 1⅔ cups. **NOTE:** To heat in glass jar remove lid and set jar in saucepan with simmering water. Heat, stirring occasionally, 20 minutes or until warm.

Crumb Pie Topping

½ cup butter or margarine, cut in
    small pieces
½ cup packed brown sugar
½ cup flour

Combine all ingredients in food processor or small mixing bowl. Blend until mixture resembles coarse crumbs. Cover top of any 1-crust pie and bake as directed.

Nectarine or Peach Sauce

2 cups thinly sliced nectarines or peaches
1 teaspoon grated orange rind
½ cup orange juice
½ cup sugar

Combine all ingredients in blender and whirl until well blended. Pour into saucepan and bring to boil, stirring, over high heat. Simmer, uncovered, 15 minutes, or until thickened. Remove from heat, cool, then chill. Good on ice cream, puddings, sherbets, etc. Store any leftover in refrigerator. Makes about 2 cups. **NOTE:** When nectarines and peaches are plentiful, make a triple batch and freeze in small containers.

Orange Sauce

2 teaspoons cornstarch
⅛ teaspoon salt
1 cup orange juice
½ teaspoon vanilla

Dissolve cornstarch and salt in ½ cup orange juice in a small saucepan. Stir over medium heat until thick and smooth. Stir in ½ cup orange juice and vanilla. Serve warm over warm pudding or pudding cake, chilled over cold pudding or cake. Makes 1 cup.

Lemon Custard Sauce

3 egg yolks
¼ cup sugar
⅛ teaspoon salt
1 teaspoon grated lemon peel
1 cup milk
2 teaspoons lemon juice, or to taste

With whisk beat yolks, sugar and salt until foamy. Combine peel and milk in small heavy saucepan; bring to boil over medium heat. Pour over egg-sugar mixture, stirring. Return mixture to saucepan; stir over low heat until slightly thickened. Remove from heat; stir in juice. Cover and chill. Serve on fresh fruit, ice cream, sherbet or gelatin dessert. Makes 1⅓ cups.

Raspberry Sauce

1 box (10 ounces) frozen raspberries, thawed
1 teaspoon cornstarch
2 teaspoons cold raspberry juice, reserved from above
Sugar (optional)
Currant jelly (optional)

Crush raspberries in a small saucepan. Dissolve cornstarch in raspberry juice in a small cup. Add to raspberries and cook over low heat, stirring, until thickened. If not sweet enough for taste, add a little sugar. Chill. Makes about 1 cup. Optional: Add currant jelly to raspberries before cooking.

Praline Topping

1 cup sugar
½ cup buttermilk
½ cup butter or margarine
1 teaspoon baking soda
1 tablespoon corn syrup
1 teaspoon vanilla

In large saucepan combine all ingredients except vanilla. Cook slowly until syrup spins a 2-inch thread (232°F. on candy thermometer). Turn into small bowl of electric mixer; add vanilla and beat at high speed until creamy.

Almond Praline Topping

½ cup granulated sugar
⅓ cup whole almonds, blanched or unblanched

Melt sugar in heavy skillet over medium heat. When sugar is amber color, stir in almonds, coating well. Carefully pour onto lightly greased cookie sheet and cool. Break praline in pieces, put in tea towel and crush coarsely with rolling pin. Makes enough to cover one pie or cheesecake.

Walnut Praline Topping

Substitute ⅓ cup walnuts for almonds in previous recipe.

Orange-Almond Topping (for pies)

½ cup sliced almonds, toasted
1 tablespoon sugar
1 teaspoon grated orange rind

Mix all ingredients and use to top pies or garnish puddings, creams, etc.

Orange-Gumdrop Flowers

Make 10 or 12 flowers, using 1 large orange gumdrop for each. With wet scissors snip an "X" at top of gumdrop almost to bottom. To form center of flower snip each quarter crosswise about halfway between center and outside. Press center together, then coat flower with granulated sugar and open petals slightly.

Vanilla Syrup

2 cups water
1 cup sugar
1 vanilla bean or 1 teaspoon vanilla
2 teaspoons lemon juice

Combine water and sugar in a saucepan. Split vanilla bean, scrape seeds loose into pan and add pod. Heat to boiling. Simmer, uncovered, 20 minutes. Remove from heat and stir in vanilla extract (if used instead of bean) and lemon juice. Makes 1½ to 2 cups, enough for a fruit compote serving six.

Lemon Syrup

⅔ cup sugar
3 tablespoons lemon juice

Mix well sugar and lemon juice. Makes enough to soak into an 8- or 9-inch square cake.

Chocolate Curls or Shreds

With heavy-duty foil shape 3½ x 2½-inch foil pan; set aside. Melt 4 to 8 squares (1 ounce each) semisweet chocolate in top of double boiler over simmering water, stirring gently occasionally. Pour into foil pan. Smooth top; let stand at room temperature until firm, several hours or overnight. With slightly warmed swivel-blade peeler or a thin-blade sharp knife, shave chocolate bar lengthwise in thin slices to form curls. With spatula carefully transfer curls to cookie sheet lined with waxed paper. Chill until firm. Store in covered container; use as needed as dessert garnish. Any leftover chocolate scraps can be remelted and reshaped into smaller bar, then shaved as above. Or shred coarse and use for garnish.

As an alternate method for making **CHOCOLATE CURLS**, run potato peeler down edge of thick milk-chocolate bar (warmed slightly by holding in hand) for desired number of curls; lift gently onto cake.

Chocolate Thins

Melt 2 squares (1 ounce each) semisweet chocolate. Pour onto cookie sheet lined with waxed paper and spread in thin layer. Freeze until firm. With sharp knife cut in diamond or desired shapes. Return to freezer. Just before serving, carefully peel away waxed paper. Use for garnish on dollops of whipped cream, cream pies, cakes or ice cream. **NOTE:** Thins soften quickly at room temperature.

Metric Conversion Tables

TEMPERATURES	INCHES TO CENTIMETERS		POUNDS TO GRAMS	
Fahrenheit°/Celsius°	Inches ("in")	Centimeters ("cm") (Nearest equivalent)	Pounds	Convenient Equivalent
180°F/82°C	¹⁄₁₆ in	¼ cm	¼ lb	115 g
190°F/88°C	⅛ in	½ cm	½ lb	225 g
200°F/95°C	¼ in	¾ cm	¾ lb	340 g
205°F/96°C	⅜ in	1 cm	1 lb	450 g
212°F/100°C	½ in	1½ cm		
225°F/107°C	⅝ in	1½ cm		
228°F/109°C	¾ in	2 cm	**OUNCES TO GRAMS**	
238°F/115°C	1 in	2½ cm		
250°F/120°C	1½ in	4 cm	Ounces	Convenient Equivalent
275°F/135°C	2 in	5 cm		
285°F/140°C	2½ in	6½ cm		
300°F/150°C	3 in	8 cm	1 oz	30 g
325°F/165°C	3½ in	9 cm	2 oz	60 g
350°F/180°C	4 in	10 cm	3 oz	85 g
375°F/190°C	5 in	13 cm	4 oz	115 g
400°F/205°C	6 in	15 cm	5 oz	140 g
425°F/220°C	7 in	18 cm	6 oz	180 g
450°F/230°C	8 in	20 cm	8 oz	225 g
475°F/245°C	9 in	23 cm	9 oz	250 g
500°F/260°C	10 in	25 cm	10 oz	285 g
525°F/275°C	12 in	30 cm	12 oz	340 g
550°F/290°C	14 in	35 cm	14 oz	400 g
	16 in	40 cm	16 oz	450 g

LIQUID MEASURE CONVERSIONS

Cups and Spoons	Liquid Ounces	Approximate Metric Term	Approximate Centiliters	Actual Milliliters
1 tsp.	⅙ oz	1 tsp	½ cL	5 mL
1 Tb	½ oz	1 Tb	1½ cL	15 mL
¼ c; 4 Tb	2 oz	½ dL; 4 Tb	6 cL	59 mL
⅓ c; 5 Tb	2⅔ oz	¾ dL; 5 Tb	8 cL	79 mL
½ c	4 oz	1 dL	12 cL	119 mL
⅔ c	5⅓ oz	1½ dL	15 cL	157 mL
¾ c	6 oz	1¾ dL	18 cL	178 mL
1 c	8 oz	¼ L	24 cL	237 mL

Index